The Blacksmith
Ironworker and Farrier

By ALDREN A. WATSON

Furniture Making Plain & Simple (with Theodora A. Poulos)
Hand Tools: Their Ways and Workings
Country Furniture
Hand Bookbinding: A Manual of Instruction
The Watson Drawing Book (with Ernest W. Watson)
The Blacksmith: Ironworker and Farrier
published by arrangement with
T & A Foxe Ltd, North Hartland, Vermont

The Blacksmith

Ironworker and Farrier

by

Aldren A. Watson

Illustrations by the Author

W · W · NORTON & COMPANY
NEW YORK   LONDON

Norton paperback edition reissued 2000
Printed in the United States of America.

The text of this book is composed in Benedictine Book, with display type set in Windsor Light.
Manfacturing by The Murray Printing Company.
Book design by Barbara Kohn Isaac.

Library of Congress Cataloging-in-Publication Data

Watson, Aldren Auld, 1917–
    [Village blacksmith]
    The blacksmith / Ironworker and Farrier by Aldren A. Watson ; illustrations by the
author.—New, expanded ed.
        p. cm.
    Reprint. Originally published: The village blacksmith. New,
expanded ed. New York : Crowell, © 1977.
    Includes bibliographical references (p.).
    1. Blacksmithing.   I. Title.
TT220.W3   1990
682'.0974—dc20   89-27554

    ISBN 0-393-32057-X pbk.

W. W. Norton & Company, Inc.
500 Fifth Avenue, New York, N.Y. 10110
www.wwnorton.com

W. W. Norton & Company Ltd.
Castle House, 75/76 Wells Street, London W1T 3QT

    4 5 6 7 8 9 0

Dedicated with
Admiration & Affection to
Peter

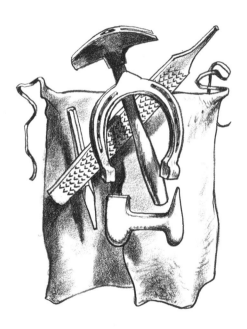

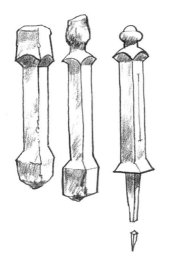

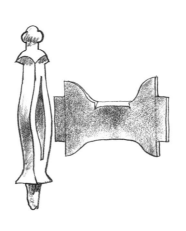

boot scraper

Preface

New England 1885-1910

The blacksmith of the turn of the century had the usual two thumbs and eight fingers; but in his case, these became an astonishing set of tools with which he manipulated to his own design an enigmatic material called iron. His work demanded a sense of timing, and a kind of resolution that separated him from other men who worked with their hands. The carpenter could knock off for lunch and later pick up his work precisely where he had left it. The wheelwright could make another spoke if his first attempt failed. The saddler did well to work his stitches with leisurely deliberation. But the blacksmith was not so lucky; his curious raw material was not static like wood and leather. His iron had a life of its own, and its behavior obliged him to make his decisions instantly. No other workman was required to carry out his tasks with such rapid-fire movements.

Functional beauty characterized almost all the iron work of the blacksmith. This alone is enough to mark him as a craftsman; yet because his products resulted from instantaneous action taken upon a substance as obstinate as wrought iron, the blacksmith deserves special recognition. Having myself struggled along a single track—to make things with my hands—I have chosen to focus on this aspect of the smith and his work rather than to stray into the equally fascinating subject of metallurgy, a branch of ironworking that has been professionally treated by well-qualified specialists. My object has been to describe as nearly as possible the life and work of the village blacksmith, who daily performed the miracle of transforming lumps of hot iron into objects of utility and grace.

For their enthusiasm and expert assistance in helping to assemble the scattered pieces in this puzzle, I am grateful to Violet S. Durgin, Reference Librarian, Forbes Library, Northampton, Massachusetts; Marion V. Bell, Enoch Pratt Free Library, Baltimore, Maryland; Dr. Paul Bryant, Boston, Massachusetts; Raymond Whitney, Hartsville, Massachusetts; and to Robert L. Crowell, whose understanding of craftsmanship has helped the work immeasurably.

A. A. W.

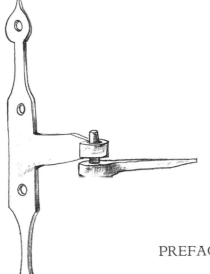

PREFACE TO THE NEW, EXPANDED EDITION

There has long been a lively interest in early American craftsmen and the significance of their work, tools, techniques, and integrity. If this preoccupation has been largely sustained by spectators, the enthusiasm of these same onlookers is partly responsible for a new trend toward active, shirtsleeve participation, on a workingman's level, in many of the traditional crafts and trades.

Among those in this trade renaissance, scores of new blacksmiths are appearing in the ranks of contemporary craftsmen. Quite a number are following the farrier's trade, for there are plenty of horses to be shod. Many more are working iron with a versatility comparable to that of the village blacksmith of long ago. The blacksmith of today is an inventive, independent workman who can shift for himself, often as much at home with the tools of a carpenter, plumber, or electrician as with his own.

The two new chapters and forty-two illustrations have been included in this edition for just such a person, and in response to wide interest, expressed in innumerable letters, for more specific information on the building of a forge and bellows. It is hoped that this new material will extend the practical usefulness of the present book.

A. A. W.

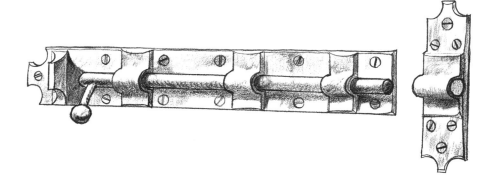

CONTENTS

The Blacksmith
Ironworker and Farrier

Prologue

Under a spreading chestnut-tree
  The village smithy stands;
The smith, a mighty man is he,
  With large and sinewy hands;
And the muscles of his brawny arms
  Are strong as iron bands.

There are few men left who can recall the once-familiar scene that inspired Longfellow to write this tribute to the village blacksmith. A large, time-weathered building stands hard by the main road in the center of the village, its huge double doors swung open to the outside. This blacksmith shop is long and rambling, with little evidence of any preliminary design: it just grew in every direction as work required and time permitted.

Inside the dim opening stands a big draft horse, pawing the oak floor planks with a front foot. A boy, perhaps fifteen years old, patiently holds the halter. The horse's ears are twitched back toward the proprietor, a strapping man wearing a leather apron. He is the blacksmith. He holds a hammer in one hand, while at his side the forge blazes cherry-red. In the background a ten-year-old boy works the great bellows, which sends air sighing into the bed of coals. Smoke curls from the fire and is sucked into the draft-hole of the brick chimney.

Now the blacksmith takes up a pair of tongs, picks a red-hot horse-

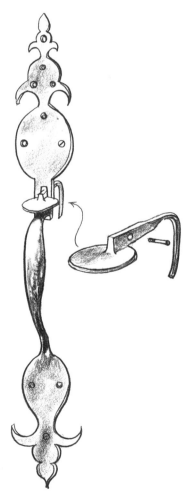

shoe from the fire, and knocks it against the anvil. A shower of pinpoint sparks scatters to the floor. Holding tongs and shoe in one hand, the blacksmith steps to the horse's side and slides his hand over the horse's rump and down his hind leg. He's a reasonable beast, this horse: when

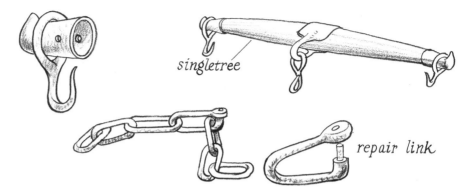

singletree

repair link

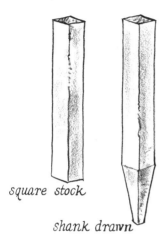

square stock

shank drawn

the smith catches hold of the long hair of the fetlock, the horse raises his foot, and the blacksmith bends it up, cradling it between his knees on the leather apron. With sure accuracy the smith lays the hot iron on the hoof; instantly, a spiral of thick white smoke rolls up. A pungent smell rises—strong, yet delicious and exciting. With the bottom of the hoof burned to an exact fit with the surface of the shoe, the smith plunges the hot iron into the nearby water tub. Steam rises hissing from the angry, bubbling water, and the iron comes out gray and cold.

The blacksmith drags his toolbox nearer with one foot; in it are his hoof-paring knife, nails, and rasp. Picking up the horse's foot again, he lays the shoe in place and sets the nails, twisting off the ends and clinching them tight. The blacksmith finishes off with a rounding stroke of the rasp, smoothing the hoof even with the iron shoe. Then he releases the horse's foot and stands up straight again. The horse tries out the feel of the new shoe, by picking it up and setting it down on the floor a few times.

This scene was as familiar as the country church to every resident of a New England that is now gone forever. The eight verses of Henry Wadsworth Longfellow's poem, published in 1841, have helped preserve the image of a craftsman who symbolized the horse-and-buggy era in America. His blacksmith, a giant of a man in flesh and spirit, once a pillar of society, has become almost a legend. Yet for one whose labor affected intimately the lives of so many people, the blacksmith has been strangely neglected by history; what little is known about him has been passed along from the fading memory of one generation to the next, losing much in the telling. Other than a handful of old prints, and a scattering of references in the pages of a few books and journals, almost nothing has been recorded that even remotely suggests the fascination of

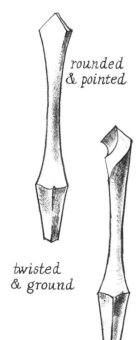

rounded & pointed

twisted & ground

the blacksmith's trade or describes his working methods. In his book
Early American Wrought Iron, Albert Sonn comments: "What manner
of man was the blacksmith of those early days, and what actually did
he make? Except in a few instances, history answers the question very
meagrely, if at all."

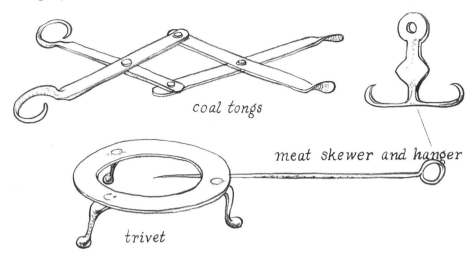

coal tongs

meat skewer and hanger

trivet

The blacksmith was no mere shoer of horses. In those long-gone good
old days he made a wide variety of things. After a horse was shod, the
smith, very likely ignoring the timid questions from the little boys
standing in the doorway, would look to his fire and move on to the
next task. Tools, hinges for a barn door, andirons for a kitchen fireplace, runners for a logging sled, new steps for the doctor's buggy,
wedges, wagon springs, door latches, pots and pans, harness hardware—
all of these useful and indispensable articles the blacksmith hammered
out of red-hot iron on his anvil. In his rude village shop he made by
hand, one at a time, nearly every metal object then in common use.
When they broke or wore out, it was the blacksmith who repaired or
replaced them.

In its cluttered way the blacksmith shop was a seemingly inexhaustible warehouse. A wooden rack along one wall stored the blacksmith's
stock of metal—sixteen-foot lengths of bar iron: square ones, round
ones, flat, oval, and rectangular ones. There were wooden kegs of horse-

shoes, arranged in handy disorder according to the smith's individual system. There were workbenches too, usually cluttered with carpenter's tools, half-finished wooden wagon parts, shavings, and very likely a few odds and ends of ironwork besides. Templates for a buggy body hung from the low rafters. In every corner were stacked iron rods, old iron parts, axles, and a host of unrecognizable items. The floor was littered with the parings from a score of horses the smith had shod that week, while around the forge and anvil leaned an impossible confusion of sledge hammers, hardies, tongs, rasps, and broken files.

What wouldn't fit inside the shop had been carted outside. Every available foot of the building's outer walls supported leaning piles of what looked like junk. Much of the old iron bore no particular resemblance to anything, yet at one time each piece had been made for a specific purpose. All were being carefully saved because they contained valuable iron or reusable bolts or both. Meanwhile, there it lay, not rusting very much, while the blacksmith's work went on. Someday he

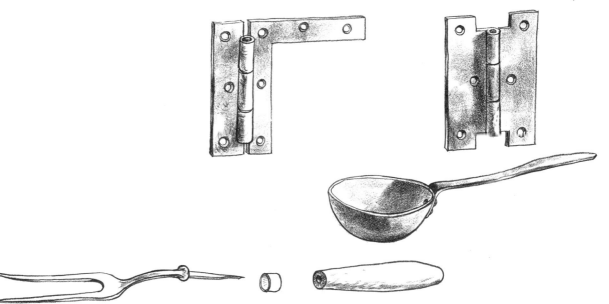

would use it all, or so he believed. And when that day came, the blacksmith would poke around his junk collection before cutting into a brand-new length of iron. Like as not he would find just the piece he needed, even if it had to be pried out from between a broken cart wheel and an old stove.

But the crowning piece of scrap-iron sculpture—the thrifty blacksmith's guild sign, as it were—was the stack of old horseshoes that might measure fifteen feet in diameter, and rise nearly to the eaves of the building. Only the horseshoes that were completely worn out went onto this pile. When he could no longer pitch any more on top, the smith sold the whole lot for a pretty penny.

4

In the Beginning

2

Blacksmithing is nearly as old as the hills that yielded the first handful of iron ore. And the first blacksmith was very probably the same man who stumbled onto this magic dirt that turned to iron in a hot fire. In this sense, he may well have been both the first ironmaker and the first blacksmith. The discovery of iron must at the same time have created the craftsman who could forge the metal into something useful.

The first recovery of iron from ore is generally conceded to have taken place about 2000 B.C., at a time when man was preoccupied with hunting and survival. Meteoritic iron had been known long before this, but because of its scarcity it had little significance. But now suddenly there was an unlimited supply of iron ready at hand, a cheap pay dirt with a hundred different uses. It had advantages over bronze: it was a simple, non-alloy metal that could be obtained, heated, and shaped with relative ease, and sharpened to an edge that could cut into a bronze shield.

The shift from bronze to iron has long been attributed to an assumed loss of the supply of tin, an essential element of bronze. Yet the suitability of iron for weapons is questionable. Pure wrought iron is practically carbon free—too soft to take a keen edge, perhaps too soft to stand the impact on bronze without bending. However, recent analysis of iron tools believed to date back to 1200 B.C. shows a surface hardness comparable to a mild steel, implying that the technique of carburization was known and used much earlier than had been supposed. Assuming this to be accurate, it may be concluded that early swords were in fact *steel*, and not simple wrought iron—which tends to question the tin theory as the dominant factor ending the Bronze Age.

It takes little imagination to visualize the sequel to this discovery: iron was certainly hammered into knives, axeheads, spears, and crude implements of agriculture—the tools of both war and peace. The discovery of iron presaged the terrible advantage that one tribe would have over weaker neighbors who were still hampered by the old, primitive equipment. The secret to this advantage would not be long in spreading around, however, for the pillaging nomads that roamed Europe and Asia inevitably left in their wake what knowledge of ironmaking they had learned.

At the same time, the knowledge of iron ores and smelting methods was spreading in other ways. Iron ores existed in great abundance in the earth's crust and over nearly all its surface, and isolated discoveries of iron occurred again and again in different parts of the world. The cycle—from discovery of ore to smelting to a more refined application of the uses of iron—was repeated many times. Yet, in spite of the isolation of these separate rediscoveries, the techniques of ironworking and the qualities of the iron itself were almost identical in every case.

Although iron tools and artifacts have been unearthed in widely scattered parts of the world, and their ages accurately determined, no records of mining methods or of smelting techniques have survived, if indeed they were even written down. Such information has been filled in arbitrarily, based upon piecemeal evidence. For example, a fourteenth-century Chinese blockprint shows a very simple blast furnace, standing about seven feet high and with an outside diameter of approximately three and a half feet. Nearby are two workmen carrying between them a basket of ore slung from a bamboo pole balanced on their shoulders. Another workman squats on the ground, apparently pulverizing the ore with a hammer, while a fourth man tends the furnace. Ironworking was known in China about two thousand years before Christ, and somewhat later in India and in the ancient countries of Phoenicia, Chal-

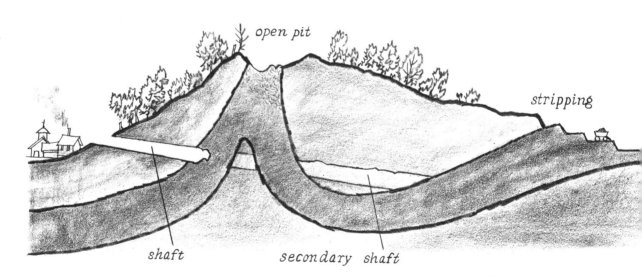

open pit

stripping

shaft

secondary shaft

dea, and Assyria. The Syrians and Egyptians are believed to have known of iron and its manipulation about as early as the Chinese. It is probable that the Greeks learned from the Egyptians; they advanced ironworking to a high degree before passing on their knowledge to the Romans.

Throughout hundreds of years of development in all parts of the world, iron was being fashioned into a variety of civilian and military products, according to the needs and habits of each society. The armor worn by Caesar's legionaries was of a different pattern from the elegant body armor of the Middle Ages. There was almost no similarity of design between an Egyptian sword and the eighteenth-century French cavalry sword. Quite naturally, iron household utensils also varied in design from country to country. Yet in all these instances the basic metal —wrought iron—and the general methods by which it was manufactured exhibited very striking similarities. By contrast, climate, latitude, altitude, and cultural habits all influenced the objects that were commonly made of wood and leather. Not every kind of tree produced wood that was suitable for these tools and objects, any more than every kind of hide could be used for shoes and water casks.

Iron played a vital part in the forward thrust of civilization. It opened the way for the invention and manufacture of complex machines that could not have been built from the traditional materials. The workability of iron gave inventors and machinists almost free rein in making machines having dozens of intricate moving parts whose accurately turned bearing surfaces would outlast their wooden counterparts a thousand times over. A dramatic and radical change in man's life followed the

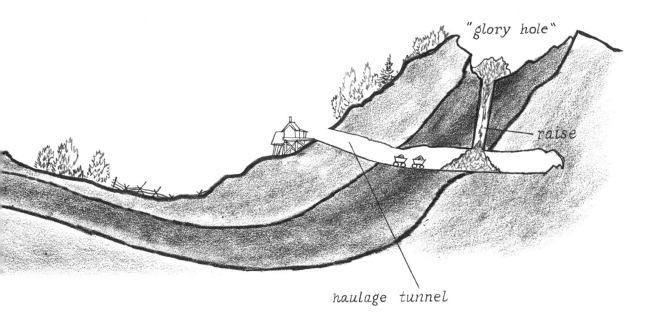

"glory hole"

raise

haulage tunnel

*Schematic diagram of
14 th century Chinese furnace*

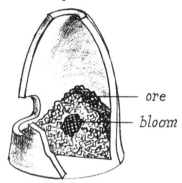

ore

bloom

rapid development of machinery that turned at high speeds, doing the work of hundreds of men using simple hand tools. It also brought mankind a new terror in the waging of war, akin to that felt by the first man who faced an enemy with an iron spear—but on a far more awe-inspiring scale. The gunsmiths, the rifle makers, the forgers of armor plate, the founders of huge military cannon, all used the same raw material and the same skills as the ironworkers who made kitchen utensils. Iron throughout its development has alternately served peace and war.

In the time of William the Conqueror, the uses for iron were so numerous that the number of blacksmiths ranked with the number of clergymen and magistrates. In one small village in England, for instance, there was enough smithing to keep six men busy. Two hundred years later, during the reign of Edward the First, there were seventy-two blacksmiths working in the Forest of Dean alone—an area roughly the size of a typical New England township. From such smithies on the continent came the massive hardware of war that took the Crusaders to the Holy Land in 1190, the horses ironshod and protected with neck armor, and their riders outfitted with articulated body armor and weapons.

The extravagant architectural explosion that punctuated the Renaissance called for the extensive ornamental use of iron. Craftsmen forged elaborate iron grilles, gates, and hardware for the adornment of public buildings, churchs, and countless magnificent dwellings. These newer, peacetime forms of ironwork were not confined to the continents of Europe and Asia. When Spain, for example, sent Cortes and his invasion armies to Mexico, she also sent a corps of blacksmiths—hardware makers equally at home with the lowly horseshoe, the weapons of conquest, and the ornamental attributes of peacetime. There are to be seen in Mexico today outstanding examples of architectural ironwork, as there are in our own Southwest and in New Orleans, to which the French brought their skill in working iron.

And at last the blacksmith came to New England. He was aboard the first ships that landed the colonists in the New World, for there were iron fittings on the vessels that needed his attention. As the new settlers went about building new communities, iron became one of the staples of colonial life. At first, though, the new land was a forbidding place. In a very real sense the New England blacksmith started from scratch, with only his skill to work with. The territory in the colonies was underlaid with ample deposits of good iron ores, but at first the early settlers were not aware of that fact. Thus, it was still necessary for the blacksmiths to import iron from Europe—notably from Russia and Sweden. Although of superior quality, imported iron was very expensive; even while working with European iron in his native England, the blacksmith had found that out. But the cost became almost prohibitive when iron was shipped across the Atlantic, for the trip required months of time, and time inflated the price. Not only that, but tons

10

of it ended up going to the bottom in ships that were never designed for such deadweight cargoes.

Under these circumstances it didn't take the resourceful and thrifty colonists long to discover iron deposits of their own. By 1722, small ironworks were springing up wherever an iron bed was found close to good water power. A thick stand of timber was another essential, for the early furnaces used charcoal for fuel and a ready supply of it was needed for the efficient working of an iron deposit. These early furnaces used ore dug from surface mines; they also used the more easily obtained bog ores that were found in the lowland swamps. While the blacksmith was compelled by necessity to use imported iron, native American iron gradually supplanted the European variety, though the shift was accompanied by constant objection and resistance from the British crown. The profit that His Majesty realized from reshipping iron to the colonies was a form of tax that would not be relinquished easily, or for that matter, very soon.

The blacksmith used the expensive European iron very sparingly: his door latches, kitchen utensils, and other hardware were forged along very simple lines. Though he knew how to turn a fine curlicue, such embellishments would have to wait; his customers, like himself, were more concerned with utility than decoration.

Gradually, however, more and more ore beds were opened from Virginia and Maryland to Connecticut, Vermont, and New Hampshire. The iron importers saw in the determined, hard-headed settlers a serious threat to what had been a very lucrative business. Furnaces were being built all up and down the east coast, and iron products were being manufactured to meet the demands of an expanding population. Iron was needed for many things in the new land, but for nothing quite as much as nails—nails and spikes to hold together the hundreds of new houses, barns, and other farm buildings. Nailmaking was a tedious business. Not

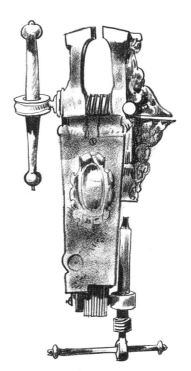

Renaissance armorer's vise

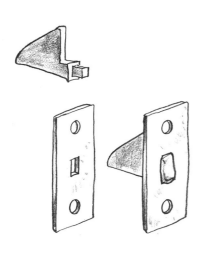

11

mushroom
spike

tack

rafter spike

trim & floor

only blacksmiths but farmers also fell to the task of supplying hundreds upon hundreds of kegs of nails of every size and description. Richard H. Hart, in his book *Enoch Pratt, the Story of a Plain Man,* describes this quaint industry:

> The firm of I. & J. Pratt [there were others] purchased consignments of Swedish and Russian iron, which was reduced to nail rods. These were sold and traded to neighboring farmers, who when not otherwise employed hammered the bars of heated iron into nails. All kinds of building hardware were scarce on this side of the water, and the finished nails commanded a good price.
>
> Nailmaking at the kitchen fireside, which occupied the winter evenings of eastern Massachusetts farmers, required but a simple equipment of anvil tools. There was always a supply of nail rods on hand. At a little smithy built within the shelter of the great kitchen fireplace these were brought to white heat, and cut into short lengths with pincers and hammer. Before the iron cooled the individual nails were shaped and headed with a few clever blows. Even the children could help with the work—the youngest at the bellows, the older boys proud to take the hammer and make the sparks fly.

The transportation problem connected with this homestead industry taxes the imagination. First, the iron bars were carried from the port of entry to outlying farm-smithies by horse and wagon. After the nail rods had been converted into nails, they were collected from the farms in the same way and put aboard coastal ships that took them to Baltimore, Philadelphia, and other ports. From these distribution points the finished nails were again carted by horse and wagon—and sometimes by pack horse—to customers scattered over an immense inland rural area. In the face of such patient stubbornness, the importers of foreign iron were defeated by the lower price of native production and eventually lost control of their profitable monopoly.

The colonial period in America is usually represented as an age of wood. This is true, yet without the myriad bits and pieces of iron, forged by hand and bent to an infinite variety of shapes, this complex wood culture would have collapsed in a heap of chips. Iron, more than any other single material, refined the attributes of civilization in America, hastened the growth of her industry, and laid the groundwork for her expansion.

While the colonies were fighting the Revolution and then pushing west across the Appalachian Mountains to the Great Plains, blacksmiths —hundreds of them—were at their forges laboriously making, one at a time, the thousands of iron parts and pieces to hold together the artifacts and equipment of life in a new land. Indeed, at this time shoeing horses was the *least* of the blacksmith's accomplishments. He was rather a general hardware maker whose skill was much in demand by the housewife, the farmer, the wheelwright, and the carriage maker. Aside from nails to hold down its floorboards, a house required several different kinds of hinges and door latches, as well as andirons, hooks, and cranes for the fireplaces, not to mention a score of special iron cooking utensils, such as ladles, dippers, skewers, knives, trivets, pots, and kettles. Out in the barn there were more hinges—much bigger ones—iron corner braces to reinforce the pegged-timber construction, and several dozen different parts that went into the wagons, sleds, buggies, and the hand-cultivating tools.

At the same time blacksmiths were engaged in other industries as well. They were forging anchor chain, bolts, eyes, and scores of special fittings for the nation's shipyards. The growing whaling industry had its own blacksmiths, turning out harpoon heads, cutting blades, and other gear necessary for killing whales and trying out the blubber. Gunsmithing was thriving too—a large industry that provided rifles, bayonets, and heavy guns for a new fleet of naval vessels. In addition, mining and quarrying, and later the printing and railroad industries, demanded the blacksmith's services.

Meanwhile, the tiresome chore of shoeing thousands of horses went on as before, a specialized branch of the blacksmith's trade that was ultimately to be the sole surviving part of his work. And all the while, blacksmiths were making or replacing their own shop tools—the hammers, pincers, punches, tongs, and swages, as well as special tools invented for specific jobs. This array of articles originated from the same raw material, worked pretty much by methods that were identical with those used in ancient times.

lath nails

finish nails

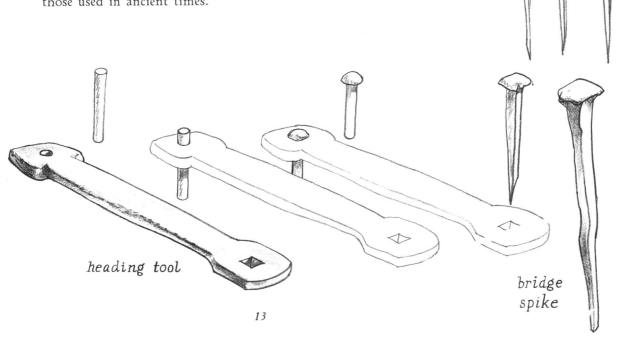

heading tool

bridge spike

13

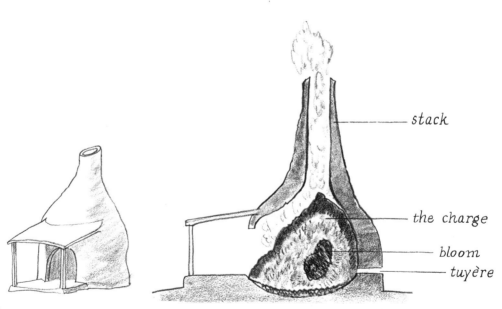

stack

the charge

bloom

tuyère

Diagram of primitive Catalan forge

Wrought Iron: Its Properties and Manufacture

3

Wrought iron was the blacksmith's raw material. It was a remarkable product—tough, long-lasting, naturally resistant to rust and corrosion, and above all comparatively easy to "work" with the simple equipment at the blacksmith's disposal. Heated in a charcoal-burning forge, the hot iron could be bent back double on itself without breaking; it withstood the stress of twisting, it could be punched and drilled, and it responded admirably to the ancient technique of welding.

In the age-old hand method of welding, far different from the oxyacetylene and electric arc welding of today, the two pieces of iron to be joined were heated to the correct temperature and fused into a single unit with a few deft strokes of the blacksmith's hammer. Of the three variants of iron, wrought iron best suited the blacksmith's purposes; it was in every way superior to cast iron and steel, both of which had been known to ironworkers for centuries. Cast iron was not pliable enough and steel was too hard for the kind of work the smith did at his anvil, and neither was as resistant to deterioration as wrought iron.

Like all the other irons and most of the other metals, wrought iron was produced by smelting ore in a furnace. The ironworks that were springing up throughout most of the colonies were supplied with ores from excavated sources and from the abundant deposits of easily recovered bog ore,* which yielded satisfactory grades of finished iron.

* Bog ore, also called bog-iron ore, was a soft ore found in marshy lowlands fed by seepage from underground. As the water leaked through iron-bearing soils and rock formations it dissolved the iron salts, which were then carried into the open air of the

Pure iron as such does not exist in a natural state. Rather, the constituents of iron are trapped in the ore; in order to combine and release them, a smelting process is required. The smelting of iron ore yields a metal which always contains some *carbon*, the exact amount of which variously influences the characteristics of the finished iron. The more carbon it contains, the harder, more brittle, and more easily fractured it will be. Thus, cast iron is a variant of the metal which has a fairly high carbon content; iron with a moderate amount of carbon is a steel; and an iron with very little carbon in its final composition is wrought iron. If purity is defined as the elimination of as much carbon as possible, then the blacksmith's wrought iron was "pure iron"—practically carbon free and containing no more than about 0.1 per cent of impurities, or *slag*. The smelting process could never completely remove all impurities: this fractional percentage became fused with the finished

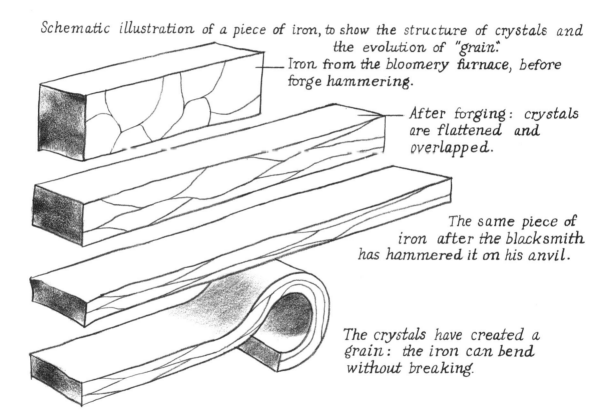

Schematic illustration of a piece of iron, to show the structure of crystals and the evolution of "grain."

Iron from the bloomery furnace, before forge hammering.

After forging: crystals are flattened and overlapped.

The same piece of iron after the blacksmith has hammered it on his anvil.

The crystals have created a grain: the iron can bend without breaking.

marsh. The decaying vegetation in the marsh, acting upon this solution, separated out the iron salts, and deposited them in the form of a reddish sludge. By this slow, continuing process of percolation, deposits of bog ore built up and became thick enough to be dug out in much the same way as peat. Provided the marsh was not drained and the growth of more vegetation was not halted, a bog renewed its supply of ore about once every twenty years.

iron, and the rest of the slag was drawn off as waste. It was the presence of these impurities as much as the low carbon content that gave wrought iron some of its superior working quality. The slag particles that remained as ingredients of the finished iron tended to form in a consistently horizontal pattern that helped create a "grain." The size and shape of the iron crystals also determined the properties of a batch of iron. Iron that was cooled rapidly at the blast furnace produced small crystals, rendering the iron hard and brittle. Slow cooling, on the other hand, produced large crystals, resulting in an iron of greater flexibility. When the iron was hammered, the crystals were flattened and hence elongated, increasing the effect of a longitudinal grain. Also, the flattened crystals overlapped one another, imparting to the iron great ductility, the ability to bend without breaking. The blacksmith may not have understood the metallurgical why and wherefore, but he was well aware of the character of his iron, and made the most of its special virtues.

The smelting process used by New England ironmakers was an ancient one. Their wrought iron was still being made in individual, small batches by the *direct process*—a one-run-at-a-time method that produced blacksmith iron that could not be matched for forging qualities by any other method. This smelting process did not undergo any real change until nearly the end of the nineteenth century.*

In the smelting of most ores, carbon serves as a *reducing agent*: it mingles with the ore in the furnace and provides the means of removing nonmetallic elements from the mixture. In general, once carbon has fulfilled this function it has no further effect on the metal. Iron is the exception, however. It can absorb considerable amounts of carbon both during smelting and afterward under special conditions. The additional amounts of carbon thus obtained profoundly change the character of the iron. Ironmakers in earlier periods had noticed this peculiarity. Now and then they found that they had accidentally made a run of cast iron or mild steel when they had intended making wrought iron. Applying their findings, they deliberately made other variants of the metal by holding wrought iron in direct contact with smouldering charcoal. This "soaking" was done in a pit lined with an insulating layer of clay. Since the variant of iron was determined by the duration of the soaking time, and guesswork was brought into play, the final product did not always measure up to a uniform standard. On the whole, a batch of wrought iron made by the direct process was a surer way of producing an iron with a predictable standard.

* Today, wrought iron is manufactured by the *fining* process by which pig iron, or cast iron, is converted to wrought iron; and by the *puddling* process, carried out in a reverberatory furnace and requiring a considerable amount of expensive hand labor. The development of new steel alloys that can be manufactured with more precise control and at less cost has made wrought iron obsolete almost to the point of being a curiosity. In fact, wrought iron today accounts for less than 3 per cent of the total steel production in the country.

17

Direct-process smelting was carried out in a stone or brick blast furnace built in the form of a square stack, wide at the bottom and tapering toward the top. Inside the stack was the *bosh,* a combustion chamber built of firebrick or slate and open at both the top and bottom. This oval-shaped compartment was insulated from the walls of the stack by a layer of sand or crushed stone. A mixture of iron ore and charcoal— the *charge*—was dumped into the top of the furnace. There were two openings at the base of the furnace, one to admit the air blast to fan the burning charge, the other permitting access to the bosh for the purpose of manipulating the iron during smelting. There was also a large door through which the finished iron was taken out.

Charcoal was considered to be a better fuel for the blast furnace and the blacksmith's forge than wood, or even coal when it came into common use.* Charcoal was a cheap fuel that burned cleanly and generated more heat than even the best dry hardwood. The vast stands of timber in the new country provided what appeared to be an inexhaustible source of readily available cheap fuel. The heat given off in the combustion of charcoal—the so-called *calorific weight*—was twice as great for charcoal as for the wood from which it was made. Charcoal produced temperatures that were even higher than those needed for blast furnace smelting. This led ironworkers to pack the charge very carefully in the bosh to avoid the possibility of accidentally producing a batch of steel.

The charcoal carbon served a dual purpose. It was the reducing agent essential to bring about the changes in the ore that would result in iron. It was also the fuel: when ignited it furnished the combustion heat necessary to raise the fire to the required smelting level—about 1200° Centigrade. The smelting of wrought iron by this process was a *reduction* process, not one of melting; the iron was never brought intentionally to the fluid or molten stage. Reduction created conditions that were ideal for the mutual attraction of iron particles in the ore on the one hand, and for the isolation of the residual impurities in the form of slag on the other.

The charge was brought to a high temperature by the burning charcoal fuel, fanned by a steady blast of air supplied by a bellows. The iron components in the ore separated into tiny crystals, which then began to unite into small metallic bodies, forming a porous, spongy mass shot through with microscopic particles of slag. These metallic bodies generally developed into a larger mass known as the *bloom*. At the same time, the impurities were massing together and generally separating from the iron. Some impurities, however, failed to separate completely. One

---

* Taking coal and wood as similar basic substances, they were converted to coke and charcoal, respectively, by heating them, out of contact with the air, until the volatile portions of the original substance had been driven off. Charcoal ignited more easily than coal and required less air blast to reach the correct smelting temperature. Coke was then virtually unknown.

substance in particular—silica—tended to remain to some extent in the bloom; these particles in the finished iron improved the composition of the wrought iron, and also raised the smelting temperature while the mass was still in the furnace.

As the bloom began to form, the ironworker prodded and worked it with a long bar so as to allow the air blast to come into contact with all parts of the mass. The spongy iron, almost as soft as putty, was then taken from the furnace and the last stage in the bloomery process begun. The bloom was taken out and subjected to repeated heavy blows by a huge tilt hammer, whose powerful impact compacted the sponge and squeezed out more of the slag. In this way the fibrous structure was brought into closer alignment, thereby increasing the strength of the iron. The ironmaker completed the final stage in the process in the nearby rolling and slitting mill. The mass of wrought iron was again brought to forging heat, rolled into thick slabs, and then slit into bars for the blacksmith.

The tilt hammer was a solid block of iron about fourteen inches square and three feet high, with a square hole in its top. It was fitted to one end of a long wooden beam pivoted in the center like a seesaw.

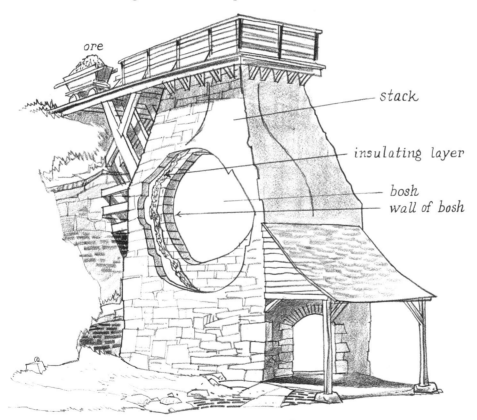

Cutaway drawing of blast furnace

19

The other end of the beam rode on the under side of a drum fitted with wooden pegs, or *dogs*. As the drum turned, each dog raised the tilt hammer and let it drop suddenly—the iron hammer striking the bloom on the anvil below. The frequency of the hammer blows was regulated by the speed of the water wheel to which the drum was geared.

The hammering that the tilt hammer gave the bloom at the iron-works can be compared to the hammering the blacksmith gave his iron at the anvil; both were part and parcel of the same refining process. The tilt-hammer forging of the bloom was essential to produce iron suitable for the final work done in the blacksmith shop. In spite of the rule that the more the hammering, the better the iron, the smith knew that iron became very brittle when hammered too many times. This very often happened, especially in forging complicated articles; iron cooled so fast that many heats were needed to complete the work. All the improvement in the iron brought about by repeated hammering would therefore have been lost unless a cure could be found for brittleness. *Annealing* was the remedy used by the blacksmith. When his work of shaping the metal was done, the smith heated the iron again; but this time he laid it up on the back of the forge to cool slowly and thoroughly in the air, instead of plunging it into water. In a piece of ironwork that

20

had required bending, the fibers lying along the outside of the bend were stretched in the process, while those on the inside were compressed. These were radical changes that set up tensions in the metal. Annealing relieved these tensions by giving the fibers time to relax and leisurely adjust to their new arrangement.

The bloomery furnace made wrought iron one small batch at a time. Once the furnace had been charged and touched off, it ran until the bloom emerged. Then the fire was drawn, the slag taken out, and the furnace made ready for a fresh charge. It was a slow process requiring a great deal of hand work, and it would have been a costly one as well but for the low price set on a man's labor in those days.

Throughout the long history of furnace operation, trial and error rather than scientific research gave ironworkers and blacksmiths an impressive fund of knowledge of the properties of wrought iron. In the last analysis one important fact stood out: wrought iron was a metal of immense virtue—provided it was properly worked. It had to be forged while cherry red; so long as the blacksmith performed his work according to the simple laws, he knew that the iron in the finished product would retain all the advantages and improvements that his forging had given it.

The Blacksmith Shop and Forge Fire

4

The forge was the heart and the anvil the soul of the blacksmith shop. The forge was a massive brick structure, carefully designed and solidly built. Resting on a stone foundation, the square brick chimney went straight up through the roof to a distance of four feet above the ridge-pole. Built off one side of the chimney was a brick, boxlike affair, waist high and measuring about five feet front to back and perhaps eight feet long. Set into the top of this brickwork, next to the chimney, was the hearth itself—a square bin the full width of the box and about twelve inches deep. The bottom of the hearth was formed by a slab of iron with a round hole in the center to accommodate the *tuyère,* or air nozzle. The tuyère was a hollow, slotted iron bulb, attached to the end of a pipe leading in from the bellows. Its function was to direct the blast of air from the bellows to one side of the fire or the other. An iron rod, running out to the front of the forge, was used to rotate and adjust the position of the tuyère. The brickwork of the hearth extended beyond the hearth to form a flat table. Here the blacksmith put finished work to cool, or laid out the pieces of iron to be forged. Near the corner of the forge was a heavy wooden crane, equipped with a traveling carriage and a pulley, by which heavy pieces of iron were lifted into the fire and out again.

The bellows was mounted behind the chimney, its air pipe leading from the bellows nozzle through the chimney, under the floor of the hearth directly to the tuyère. In shape this bellows resembled its tiny counterpart that stood by the kitchen fireplace, but the smithy bellows

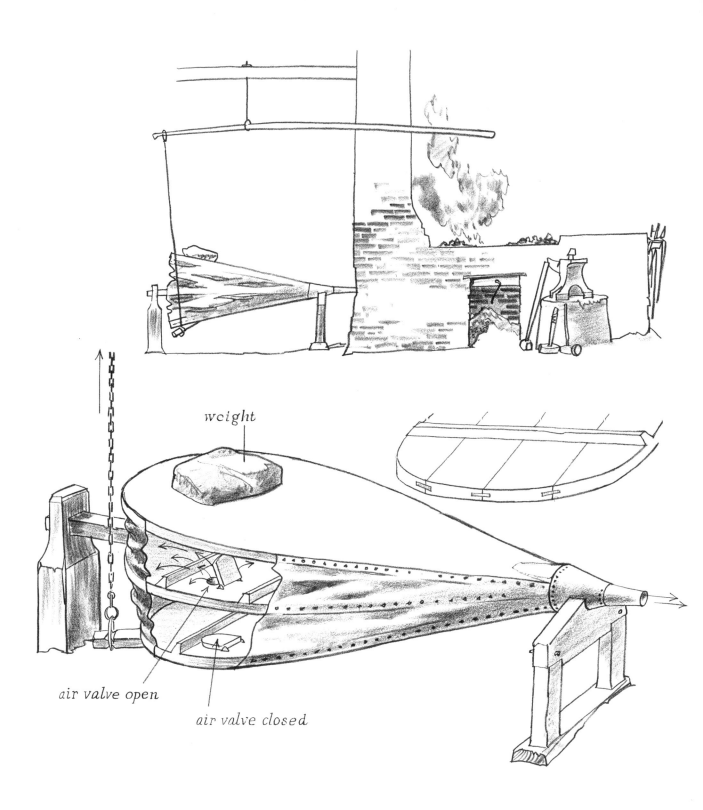

weight

air valve open

air valve closed

was a gargantuan leather lung about eight feet long and four feet across its widest part. Built on a wooden framework of flat paddles, it had a stationary middle paddle—held up at the nozzle end and secured at the back end to a wooden post set in the floor. The top and bottom paddles were movable, hinging at the small end. Accordionlike leather sides, closely nailed to the edges of the three paddles, created an airtight pair of chambers. A small valve in the middle paddle opened only on the upstroke of the lower paddle, which was moved by a chain attached to an overhead lever pole. A large stone laid on top of the bellows kept a constant pressure on the air in the upper chamber. As the lower chamber was squeezed shut, air was forced from it into the upper chamber, where, being under pressure of the stone weight, the valve closed and immediately trapped the air. The only exit now was through the nozzle and into the tuyère. And thence it went in a smooth stream, instead of by the jerky, huff-and-puff gusts created by a single-chamber bellows. With the overhead lever a blacksmith could even manage to work the bellows alone, though most smithies employed a youngster for the job. If the blacksmith needed more heat he had but to pump the lever a bit more vigorously; otherwise an occasional stroke was enough to keep a gentle wind blowing.

The exact location of the anvil was an important matter, for every piece of iron had to be heated at least once or twice, and usually four or five times. Iron cools quickly to the point where it can no longer be worked; hence the anvil had to be close to the fire. No less critical was the height of the anvil, a matter determined by the size of the man who was to use it. If the anvil was too high, even the mightiest smith could wear himself out swinging his hammer; if too low, the hammer could never strike the surface of the anvil squarely. Ideally, the bottom of the blacksmith's natural hammer stroke just matched the height of the anvil. The general rule was to place the anvil so that the blacksmith standing in front of the forge need make only a quarter-turn away from it to put himself within hammer distance of the anvil. Again to save time, and to prevent too much cooling of the hot iron, the horn of the anvil pointed toward the forge to the blacksmith's left, if he was right-handed.

The anvil was mounted on the top end of a post buried four or five feet in the ground. If the blacksmith was clever, he had done some careful calculating before digging a hole that deep and then upending the heavy chunk of green timber into it. Once he dropped the post into the hole, he would find it an embarrassing and difficult chore wrestling it out again to dig a bit deeper. The anvil itself was an iron giant with a base that forked out into four legs, secured by quarter-inch iron rods driven into the post and bent down over the legs. Sometimes an iron hoop was driven down around the top of the post to hold the timber tight and to prevent its splitting while it was drying out. Once he had finished this heavy labor, the smith was little interested in doing it all

25

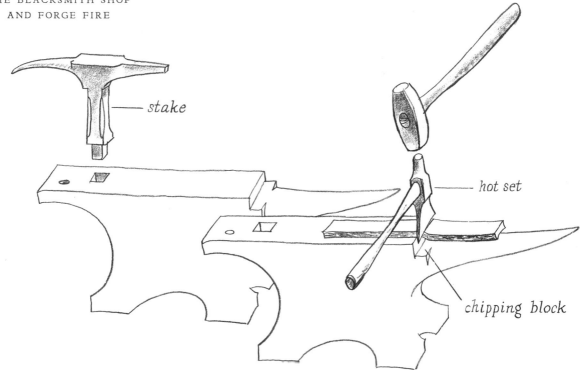

stake

hot set

chipping block

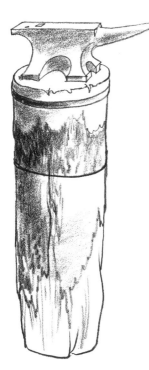

over again. But neither did he want to spend his days working at a poorly fitted anvil. So he measured well, and then checked his arithmetic before starting to dig.

Firmly anchored to the layer of hardpan beneath the smithy floor, this two-hundred-fifty-pound block of iron was an awesome sight. It measured about five inches across, was twenty inches long, and had a graceful sixteen-inch horn curving up from one end. Its top face was a slab of tool steel welded to the wrought iron base.

Two holes were cut into the *heel*, or back end of the anvil, from the face through to the underside. The *hardy hole* was a square one, made to fit the square shanks of the blacksmith's many forging tools. The other—called the *pritchel hole*—was about three-eighths of an inch round. It was used for punching jobs, such as knocking the old nails out of horseshoes. The *chipping block* was made of wrought iron; in cutting off a piece of hot iron, the work was laid out over this softer section so that the sharp edge of the chisel was unharmed when it struck through to the chipping block.

An especially good anvil was made and installed with two added refinements. In almost every forge operation, the blacksmith had first to *draw* the iron to make it thinner, or wider. To make this repetitious task easier, the best anvil had a slightly convex face. The second refinement

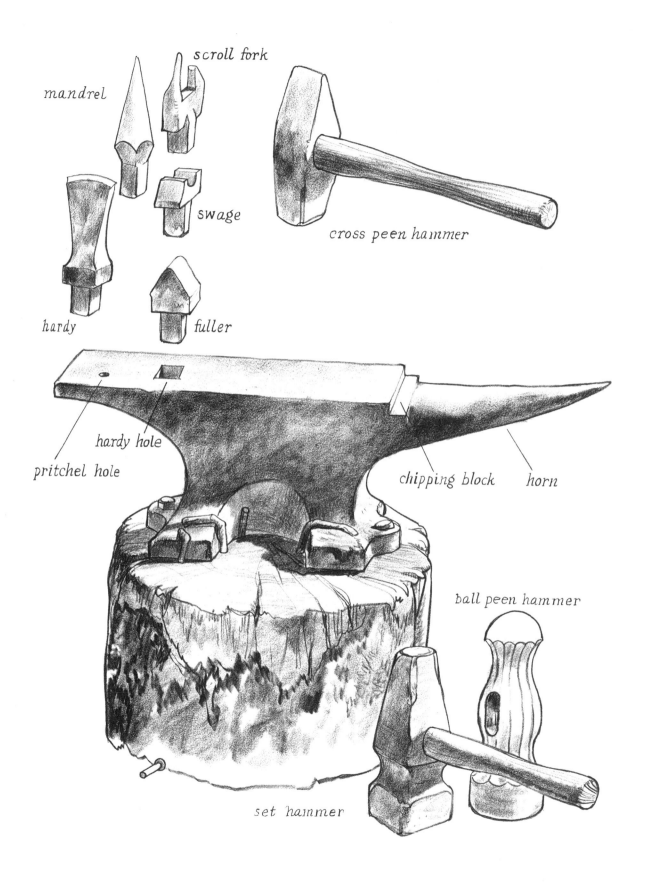

mandrel

scroll fork

cross peen hammer

swage

hardy

fuller

hardy hole

pritchel hole

chipping block

horn

ball peen hammer

set hammer

concerned the installation of the anvil: loose slivers of scale always erupt on the surface of heated iron. Ordinarily, the smith rapped the hot iron against the side of the anvil to knock the scale loose. But if the anvil was mounted with a slight tilt, its face pitched away from the smith a bit and most of the scale slid off by itself under the first hammer blows.

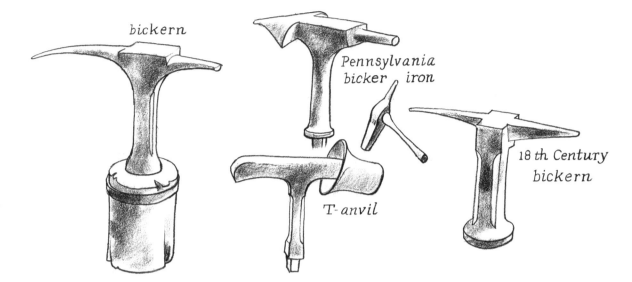

bickern

Pennsylvania
bicker iron

T-anvil

18th Century
bickern

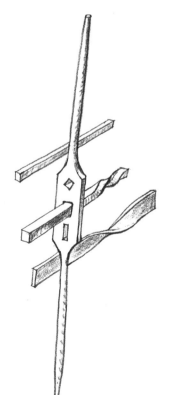

Some village blacksmith shops had another, much smaller anvil, mounted in the same fashion but out of the way alongside the bellows. Variously called a *bickern, beck iron,* or *bicker iron,* it was a slender, tapered anvil with a long horn pointing downward and a heel about an inch and a half square. It was a handy anvil for forging round and hollow work, such as kitchen pots and utensils. An anvil tool called a *stake,* which fitted the hardy hole of the regular anvil, gave the smith about the same working surfaces as the bickern. These two tools were practically identical copies of the stake and bickern used by European armorers in the Middle Ages.

Nearer the center of the blacksmith shop, but still within easy reach of the forge, was a heavy iron vise mounted on yet another sunken post. Long iron bars to be twisted were clamped by one end in the vise, and the smith manipulated the hot iron with a *twisting bar.*

The foot-treadle grindstone, by far the best sharpening machine ever invented, was an important tool in the smithy. In the course of his career the blacksmith might grind six inches away from its diameter and wear out the legs of several boys in the process. Yet to this day it is preferred over the high-speed bench grinder, which may overheat and draw the temper from the tips of cutting tools.

Two or three workbenches and a *slack tub* for quenching hot iron completed the usual list of shop equipment. One bench was set aside for

28

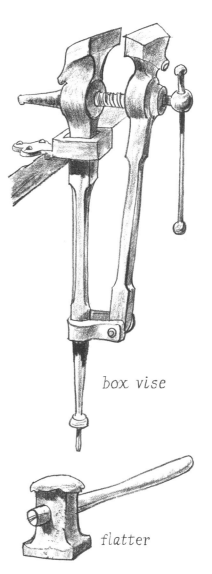

box vise

woodworking repairs on wagons; the tools the smith needed were there
—hammers and saws, chisels, brace and bits, planes, a square, draw-
knives and spokeshaves. If he did any amount of wagon work he would
also have a small foot-treadle lathe. Buggies, wagons, and carts were
being factory made at the turn of the century, but customers who lived
two or three hundred miles from the factory brought broken wheels to
the blacksmith. He often had to make new spokes, rims, and occasionally
an entire wheel, hub and all.

There was another section of a bench for finishing work. Since the
forging left slight imperfections and rough spots on most of the work,
such pieces were taken to this bench for the final touches. It was fitted
out with a husky, iron box vise and the usual clutter of files, tin shears,
punches, a cold chisel, and a small *flatter* for smoothing out rough places.

The blacksmith may have trusted his helper to get the forge ready
for work. But probably he was content to let him get up before day-
break and split a chunk of dry pine and another of seasoned oak, then
scoop up a few handfuls of curly wood shavings from the floor, and
fill the hearth with charcoal from the bin. The blacksmith may very
well have preferred to have all this done—and his tools laid out—before
his own work day began.

But when it came to actually building and lighting the fire, that was
a privilege the smith reserved for himself. It was too important to the

flatter

29

day's work to be left to a helper. The first task was to clean out the old fire right down to the tuyère. Into this cavity—no bigger than a teapot—the smith packed a deep layer of the dry wood shavings. Then he laid on some splinters of dry pine, leaving air spaces between them, and finally a good layer of oak sticks. The hardwood would hold the heat long enough for the charcoal to catch. Then the smith lit the fire. The shavings burned fast and soon the pine was crackling and beginning to ignite the oak. As the pocket of kindling settled into the hole the oak caught fire; the blacksmith then gently raked charcoal in over the fierce little fire.

When the charcoal was burning well, the smith caught the bellows lever and pumped a bit of draft into the hearth. The fire began to glow red. The wood kindling was gone by now and the fire had come to life. The smith could look to his tools and to the work that lay ahead. His helper sprinkled water on the charcoal around the edges of the fire to keep it from spreading too far, for the blacksmith's fire did not need to be any bigger than a dinner platter, since most of his work involved heating relatively small pieces of iron. As the charcoal burned out and turned to gray ash, fresh fuel was raked in from the edges; it was never piled directly on top. When ready for work, the fire was a mound of bright red charcoal, the interior of which was nearly white; the whole mass was somewhat loose, permitting the air blast to work through it. Depending on how vigorously the bellows was pumped, the fire offered a wide range of temperatures, from a quiet dull red to a raging white intensity. The smith was a color expert when it came to his fire; he recognized the temperature change indicated by each color and knew how to manipulate the fire to achieve the heat he wanted.

When he wanted a long fire to accommodate something as long as a buggy axle, the blacksmith packed two sides of the fire with fresh, wet charcoal and left the other sides open so that the fire would burn toward the ends. At the same time he removed bricks intentionally left loose in the rim of the forge to allow long pieces of iron to hang over the sides. The bellows was used sparingly. Too much air blast quickly ate up the charcoal in the center of the fire, leaving it *hollow*; that is, with the burned-out fuel loosely stacked and with cold air spaces between. A good fire was a close-packed mass of live red coals; iron thrust into a tight fire was in close contact with the coals on all sides and would take heat uniformly.

During a work lull or when he had to leave the forge, the smith stuck a piece of old dry hardwood into the fire to hold the heat of the fire until he returned. Old wagon spokes and other small chunks of hickory, ash, oak, and maple were saved for this purpose. Even when the fire had apparently died out cold, it could often be revived by sprinkling a handful of sawdust on the coals. As long as the coals were hot enough to "smoke sawdust," the fire could be brought back.

At the end of the day blacksmiths often left their forge fires alive for the night. The coals were packed down gently around a stub of apple wood and a bucket of wood ashes was mounded over the fire to trap the heat. A fire that was banked with ashes in this way could be opened up the next morning and brought to working heat in a few minutes.

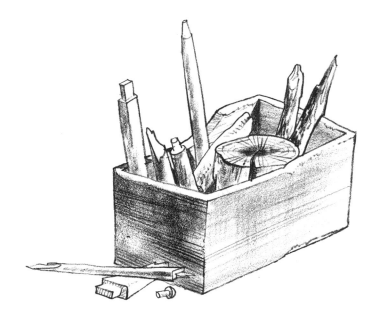

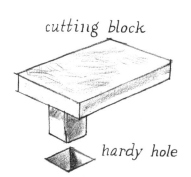

cutting block

hardy hole

bending fork

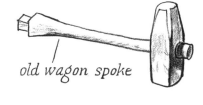

old wagon spoke

Working at the Forge

5

*Stand close to the anvil. Watch the black-
smith's hammer for signals. When the blow
is delivered draw the sledge quickly toward
you before starting to raise it again. Always
strike the work in the same place and at the
same angle as the smith is striking.*

In this quotation from his book *Blacksmithing: A Manual for Use in
School and Shop,* R. W. Selvidge points a finger at a very important
aspect of the blacksmith's trade. Selvidge's language is precise, and a bit
more elegant than the smith himself would have used, but the message
is just as clear. For the blacksmith, in spite of all his fine equipment and
a binful of charcoal, couldn't have forged anything much more elaborate
than a few pairs of small butterfly hinges without a helper. Farmers
brought in work that was heavy, cumbersome, and often dangerous for
one man to attempt alone, especially when the iron to be worked was
made red-hot. Handling wagon axles, tire irons, and sled runners was
physically beyond even the beefiest blacksmith. Besides, most anvil work
involved the simultaneous use of two or three tools and four hands.
Alone, the smith couldn't hold a piece of hot iron in the tongs, guide
a shaping tool, and at the same time swing an eight-pound sledge.

The blacksmith's helper was known as a *striker.* He stood facing the smith on the other side of the anvil, ready with his heavy sledge to lay on blows as the blacksmith directed. Neither spoke a word—there was too much noise for conversation. By lightly tapping the spot with his small hammer, the blacksmith showed his striker where he wanted the sledge to strike. A good striker was expected to use the sledge left- or right-handed with equal ease, delivering the blows from any angle and placing them with unfailing accuracy on the head of the tool the blacksmith held. He had to hold to a regular rhythm and keep his eyes open; when the smith tapped a different spot, or rotated the work on the anvil, the striker was to be ready for just a momentary pause and then a full-sized blow. In this exacting teamwork, the striker knew what movements were coming and anticipated them. When the smith wanted the striker to stop he used the universal signal: a light tap of the hammer on the anvil to one side of the work.

It was the striker's job to assemble whatever tools the smith would need for a job, and have them laid out ready at hand. In the blacksmith's long day, filled with a dozen different tasks each requiring scores of hammer blows and constant changing of tools, there wasn't time to run around the shop hunting for them while a piece of hot iron lay cooling on the anvil. A striker worth his salt had to have about the same general knowledge of ironwork as his smith. There were times when he took over the anvil while the smith was away from it, working on a special job; and he had to know how to keep the fire and take care of a dozen other things while the blacksmith was absent.

Most blacksmith shops hired one boy—sometimes two—who took care of the chores of pumping the bellows, turning the grindstone, sweeping up, and running errands. It was the old apprentice pattern still in operation, but without the formal or legal arrangements the system originally involved. The sons of blacksmiths learned the trade at this sort of work and were soon promoted to shoeing horses, frequently having to start out on the ornery ones. Maybe this was looked on as an initiation; more likely it was just that nobody else wanted the job. When the young blacksmiths had gained enough skill and experience they became strikers, and eventually took over the father's shop or started their own.

As the blacksmith and his striker worked, the melodious, ringing tap-tap-tap of the smith's hammer, alternating with the heavier clang of the sledge, set up a vibrating rhythm that could be felt in the trembling ground beneath the anvil and heard for half a mile down the road. Every now and then the tempo was punctuated by the sound of hot iron plunging into the water tub, and at longer intervals the pitch changed as a new set of tools was put to work on a different task.

The blacksmith's collection of tools seemed endless. He accumulated them in ever-increasing variety, and rarely threw one away even after it was worn out. Iron was too costly, and the day might come when he could make a new tool from two old ones. His everyday tools—hammers, swages, fullers, and punches—were in steady use and lay on a low

bench behind him near the anvil. A scattering of others hung on the forge rack, lay on the floor, or stood against the wall, perhaps to be used once or twice a year—perhaps not for another five. For the blacksmith was an innovator; he designed and made new tools for special jobs, tools that had no names and that were never duplicated or copied by a factory. For nearly every small hand tool the smith had a matching counterpart with a longer handle so he could work at arm's length, standing clear of the striker's swinging sledge.

The smith's tools eventually took on something of his own personality. Repeated use gave them a feel and a heft that suited him. Every

TONGS

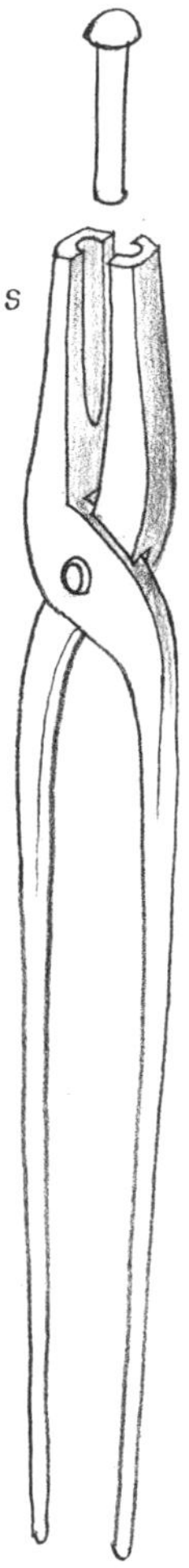

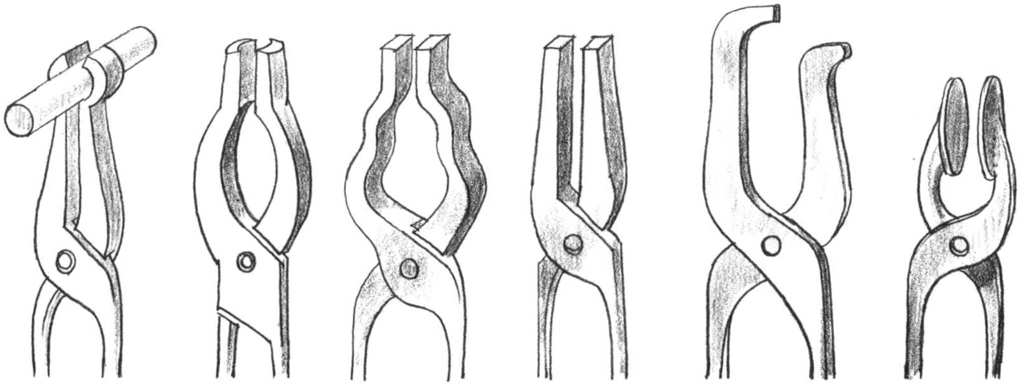

link   hollow bit   anvil or pick up   hoop tongs   horseshoe

cone mandrel
for shaping
iron rings

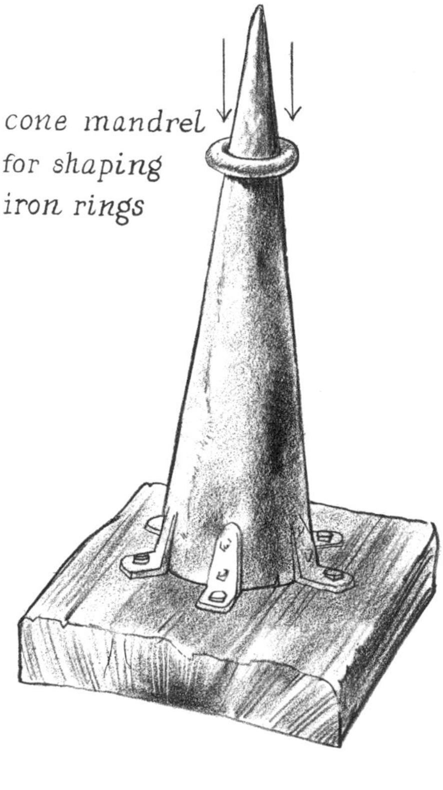

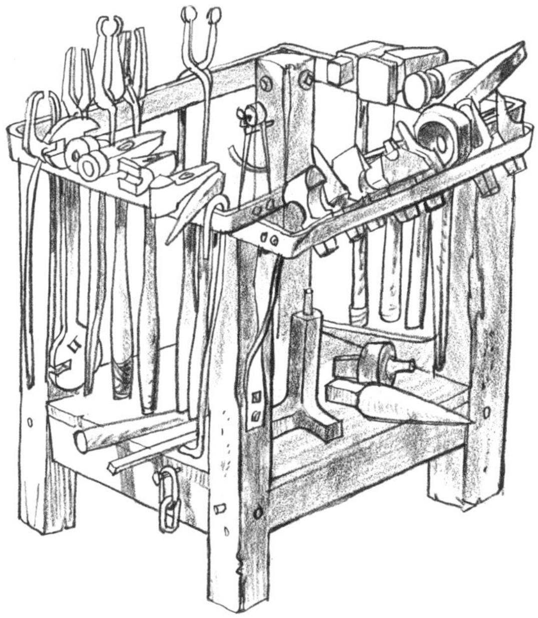

36

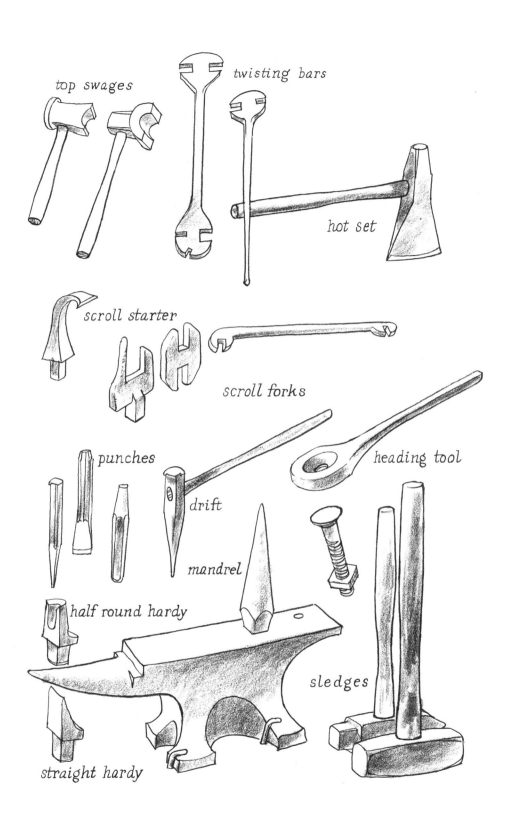

top swages

twisting bars

hot set

scroll starter

scroll forks

heading tool

punches

drift

mandrel

half round hardy

sledges

straight hardy

tool and its wood handle wore to his grip, so that in the press of working at the anvil he could pick up a tool without looking for it, or at it. He recognized each one by its particular "feel." When a handle broke it was a minor disaster, since it would take the smith a long time to get used to a new one. Even after the factories began turning out blacksmith tools, the smith often preferred to make his own and to fit his own handles into them, just to get the length that matched his arm, the diameter that filled his grip, and the weight that suited his stroke. Blacksmiths saved old wagon spokes for this purpose, for they were well-seasoned pieces of good hardwood.

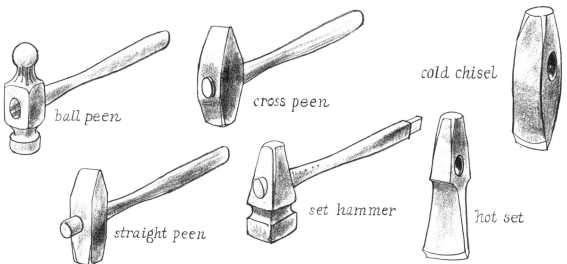

ball peen

cross peen

cold chisel

straight peen

set hammer

hot set

The work of the smith and his striker was disciplined throughout by exact timing. As soon as iron was put into the fire it began to "take" heat, readily soaking it up from the blazing charcoal. At first the iron looked dull red, but as its temperature increased its color changed to cherry red, then to yellow, and finally to forging color—a bright lemon yellow. Now was the moment to take it out of the fire before it reached white heat, for at that nearly fluid stage it would easily burn; at white heat small particles of molten iron exploded and were consumed as they showered back into the fire. As the smith withdrew the iron, the striker stood ready at the anvil, both hands gripping his sledge, one foot extended a half step, waiting to raise his arms for the first blow. When it fell, it would be the first of half a hundred—some quite light, others heavy, some delivered with full power. Whatever the tool the blacksmith held ready, the striker measured his blows to match the smith's signal, whether the task at hand was to take up ten minutes or the whole forenoon.

The variety of steps in the blacksmith's anvil work can be grouped under eight general headings; taken all together, they make up what is termed *forging*. Not even the simplest article could be completed in one

38

operation. Forging was a series of controlled steps, rapidly executed in a certain sequence, interrupted only long enough to thrust the work back into the fire to bring it again to forging heat. Though most tasks needed only three or four of these operations, some required all of them. Making an ordinary horseshoe, for example, called for all but welding and tempering.

Cutting. In its red-hot, pliable condition, iron could be cut as easily as thick leather. The smith had several *hot sets;* these were cutting tools with wood handles, much like hatchets. One good blow of the hammer on the head of the set would drive it through a piece of half-inch iron.

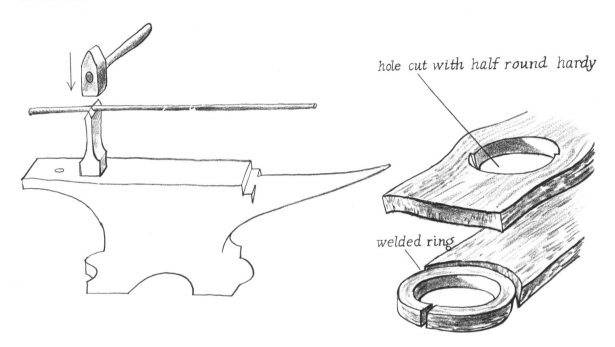

hole cut with half round hardy

welded ring

The stubby cutting tools that fitted into the hardy hole of the anvil were called *hardies;* some were straight, others half-round for use in cutting large holes. The iron to be cut was laid on top of the hardy so that the hammer blows fell on the work itself. The smith could do this alone, whereas using the sets required the striker's help. Two carefully placed cuts with the half-round hardy would make a satisfactory hole, but where a much stronger one was needed, the smith first welded an iron ring, then welded that into position with the rest of the work. As its name suggests, the *cold chisel* was handy for cutting thin pieces of cold iron, or for shearing off rivet and bolt heads. The hacksaw was also very often used to cut small-dimension iron stock and to perform minor cutting at the finishing bench.

Fullering. This routine work, also called *drawing,* was the means of making iron of a large dimension smaller. For example: The flat blade of a garden hoe was drawn out to taper its bottom edge; an axe whose cutting edge needed reshaping was heated and drawn to stretch the metal to the size of the original axehead. As the carpenter planes and smooths a piece of wood stock before making something of it, so the blacksmith fullered his iron before he forged it. The extra bit of hammering compacted the iron and strengthened it—a step necessary to the preparation of stock bar iron.

The smith fullered small pieces of iron by simply hammering the work as it lay on the face of the anvil. More ambitious jobs required a pair of special tools called *fullering irons*, or *fullers*, and the help of the striker. With his tongs the blacksmith held the cherry-red iron across the bottom fullering iron, which was set solidly in the hardy hole. The anvil took the brunt of the hammer blows. The smith guided the

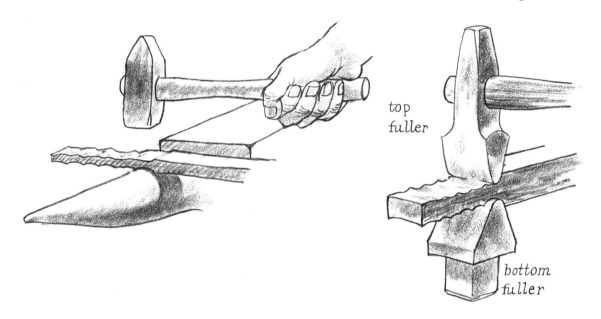

top
fuller

bottom
fuller

top fuller with his other hand while the striker clouted the head of the tool a clanging blow with his sledge. Each blow squeezed the iron out, making it longer and thinner. Fullering was started on the end and worked toward the center. After each blow the work was moved over ready for the next one. Because of the structure of iron, most of the stretching took place with the grain, very little change occurring in the cross grain, or width, of the iron. A long piece of iron had to be heated several times; when completely fullered it was heated once more and smoothed out with a *flatter*. There were a number of parts and pieces balanced on the anvil during fullering, and if the striker missed, the consequence was apt to be disastrous. The impact of the sledge might hurl the red-hot iron into the air and send the tools flying in every direction.

Drawing down, or fullering, a piece of large round bar to a smaller

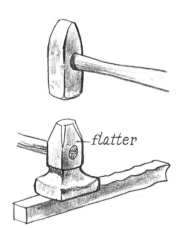

flatter

40

diameter was never done with so-called round-and-round forging because this method broke down the interior structure of the iron and
ruined the metal. Instead, the blacksmith reduced it first to a square,
then to an octagonal shape by steady hammering along all the edges.
After this, it was a simple matter to continue this gradual reduction by
hammering out all the edges of the octagonal piece until the iron re-
gained its shape as a round bar, but of a smaller diameter.

When uniformity of thickness or exact diameter was important, as in
the making of a batch of bolts, the smith used a pair of matching *swages*
whose inside, half-round surfaces produced identical shanks. The big
chunk of iron called a *swage block,* with its variety of holes and cutouts,
gave the blacksmith the means for shaping hollow and curved articles,
such as ladles and bowls.

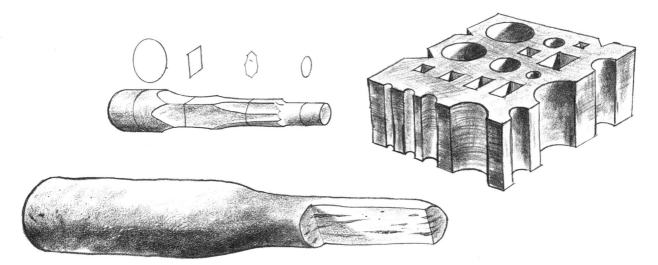

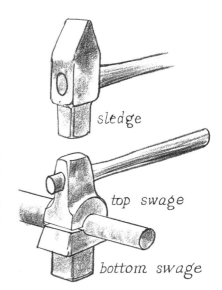

fracturing of round bar due to improper fullering

In all fullering, the length of the iron was increased, a fact the smith
took into account when measuring and cutting his iron to begin with.
The same principle of fullering is carried out today in the rolling mill,
where a billet of red-hot iron is stretched, shaped, and formed during
several passes between the rollers, finally emerging as, say, a finished
steel railroad rail.

Upsetting. The blacksmith used this forge operation to thicken, or
bulge, iron. It enabled him to bunch up some of the metal into an extra
thickness in certain places, before forging the work on the anvil. The
smith always upset both of the pieces of iron to be welded, thus gaining
extra iron where needed so that the finished weld would be the same dimension as the rest of the work. For instance, the thumbpiece on a door
latch was made from a bulb of iron upset on one end of the work, and

sledge

top swage

bottom swage

41

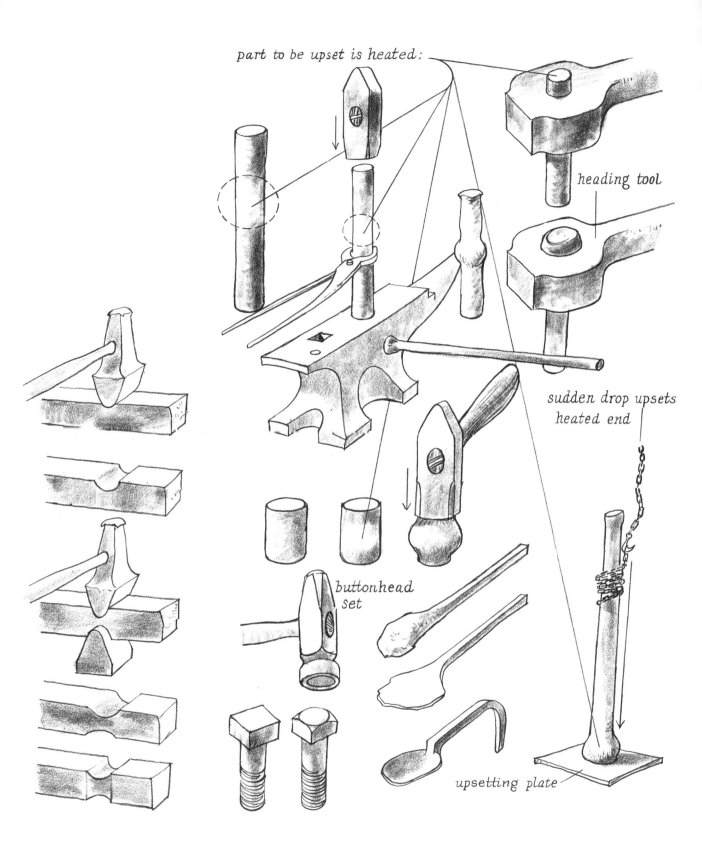

part to be upset is heated:

heading tool

sudden drop upsets
heated end

buttonhead
set

upsetting plate

then flattened. Just how much iron had to be gathered in the upset portion was determined by the particular work at hand and by the blacksmith's judgment; he needed enough but not too much. A worn-out axehead could be repaired by first upsetting, or pushing back, the iron along the cutting edge. With this extra iron the smith could reshape it. He also used upsetting extensively in making bolts. A piece of round bar iron was cut to length and one end heated to a cherry red. The smith then slipped it into a *heading tool* with the hot end projecting above the top of the tool. Resting the cold end of the iron on the anvil, the smith gave the hot end a good wallop with his hammer, which squashed the soft iron into a bulb. He could then give the head its final shape by laying a *buttonhead set* on the head for one last hammer blow.

When larger pieces of iron were upset, the red-hot end was "danced" on the face of the anvil, or against the side of it, in a battering-ram motion, the weight of the iron alone being enough to provide the necessary impact.

Bending. The blacksmith made bends of every description on most of the work he did. Bending set up a great deal of stress in the iron, however, its parallel granular structure being suddenly forced into a radically different alignment. Therefore, cold bending was seldom used except on very small articles where strength was not a critical factor. Depending on the type of bend and the thickness of the iron, the blacksmith used the sharp edge of the anvil, the horn, the bickern, or some of the special *scroll forks,* which were useful in starting bends. A bend sharp as a right angle was generally accomplished in two or three heats of the iron. These successive stages eliminated the risk of bending the iron when it was too cool, which would ruin its strength.

Welding. By this ancient process, the blacksmith joined two or more pieces of iron into one. He could make strong right-angle corners, or weld several layers of iron into one thick chunk. It had little in common with the modern welding methods except that they all accomplish the union of pieces of iron.

The iron was first heated to white heat. In this near-fluid state the pieces actually fused and became one. But preparation and care were es-

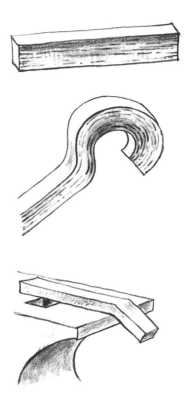

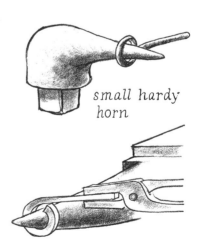

small hardy horn

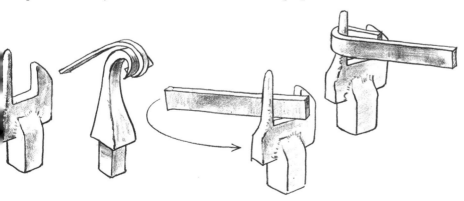

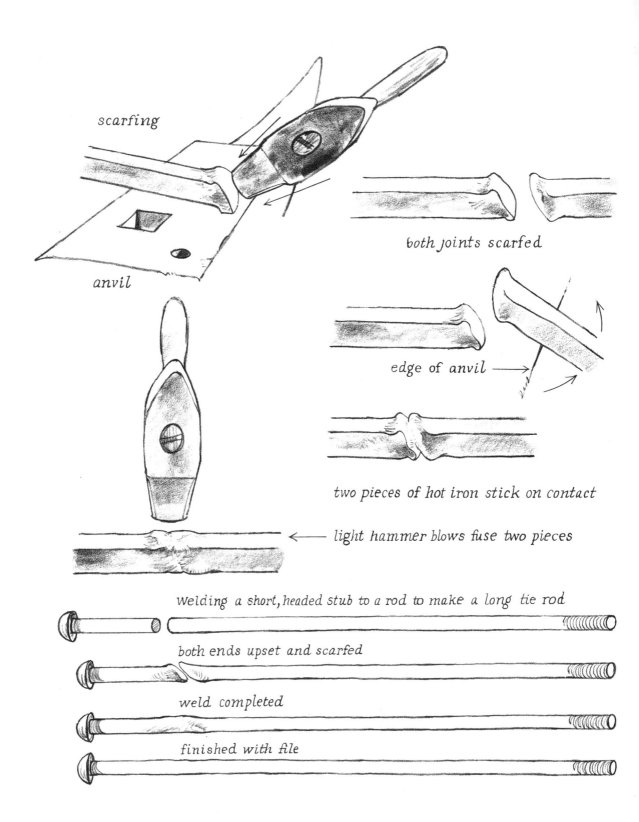

scarfing

anvil

both joints scarfed

edge of anvil →

two pieces of hot iron stick on contact

← light hammer blows fuse two pieces

Welding a short, headed stub to a rod to make a long tie rod

both ends upset and scarfed

weld completed

finished with file

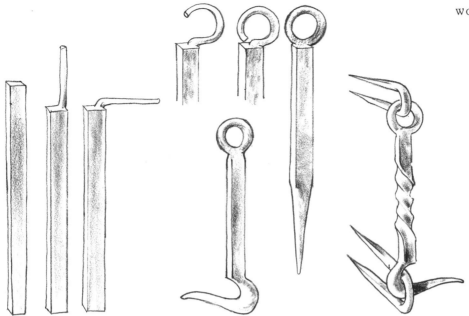

sential to good welding: both surfaces had to be in complete contact, and of course air bubbles or pieces of scale in the joint made this impossible. To avoid this and assure a tight closure of the joint, both pieces of iron were first *scarfed*: the ends of the pieces were upset and both surfaces were slightly beveled and rounded. As a further guarantee against scale in the weld, the blacksmith sprinkled a little *flux* on the two pieces of iron as they lay in the fire. Flux lowered the melting point of scale, sand being used for wrought iron and machine steel, and borax

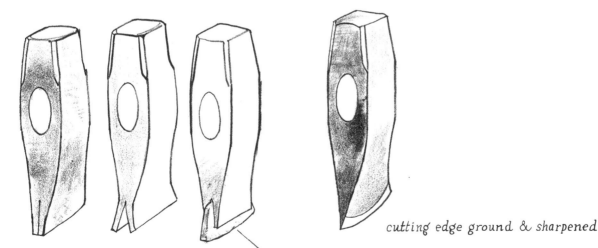

edge split & spread   wedge of tool steel welded in split   cutting edge ground & sharpened

45

for tool steel. By the time the iron reached white heat, a large percentage of the scale would have melted. The white-hot pieces of iron were then taken to the anvil. The smith held one piece in his tongs, flat on the anvil face. He laid the other piece at an angle over the edge of the anvil, tipping it up until it touched the first. The semimolten iron surfaces stuck to each other on contact, and with a light stroke of his hammer the smith started the weld. As the hammer strokes worked on the scarfed ends, the joint was "rolled" shut, squeezing out air and scale and allowing both surfaces complete contact. The best welding was done with a few swift strokes; belaboring the work was sure to ruin it.

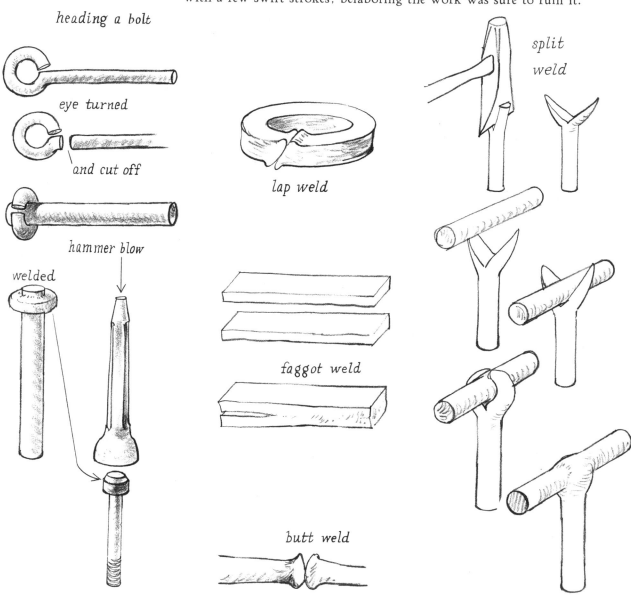

heading a bolt

eye turned

and cut off

hammer blow

welded

lap weld

faggot weld

butt weld

split weld

46

If the welding had been done correctly the work was now as strong as a single piece of iron. If it failed, however, the practical smith took new stock and began again, for he knew that the difficulty of getting iron to weld increased with each additional attempt.

Depending on what he was making, the smith cut his iron to make one of several types of joints. The lap weld, faggot weld, cleft or split weld were selected according to need and durability, as were the T weld, and jump welding. In all these types of joints, the welding principle was the same, and the blacksmith prepared his iron with the same concern for the exclusion of air and scale.

corner weld

end of bar welded into corner, surplus cut off

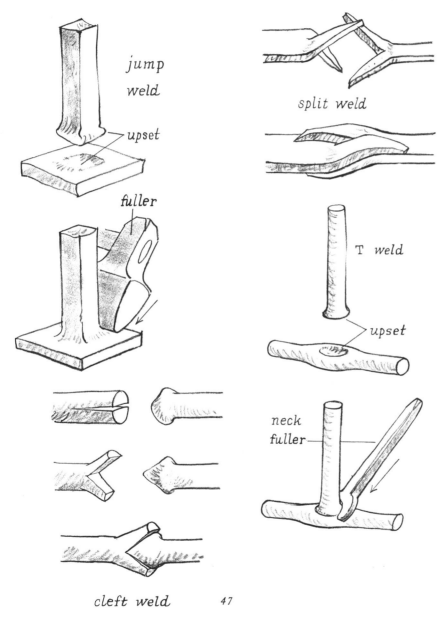

jump weld

upset

fuller

split weld

T weld

upset

neck fuller

cleft weld   47

drift punch

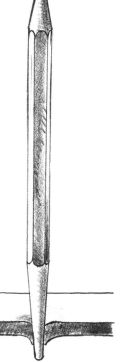

Punching. The simplest way the blacksmith had of making holes in iron was to punch them. Hot iron punched easily, and it was much faster than even a hand drill. The iron was heated to a light red and laid flat on the anvil. With one good hammer blow the blacksmith drove the punch deep *into* the iron, but not through it. The punch left a mark on the other side of the work—a guide for the final punch. The work was turned over and the punch mark positioned over the hardy hole. Another good blow drove out the plug, or button of iron, and it fell through to the floor, a method that prevented striking the anvil and damaging the working end of the punch.

A large hole was started with a small punched hole, into which the blacksmith placed a big *drift*—a tapered punch with a long handle. By working this drift back and forth, and calling on the striker for an oc-

Punching clear through in one stroke leaves a large burr

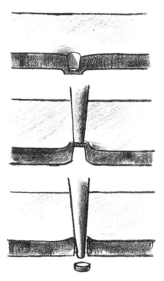

Punching from both sides makes a cleaner job

casional hammer blow, the smith could enlarge the hole to the full diameter of the drift. This method swelled the iron around the hole, but did not in any way diminish the ultimate strength of the finished work.

Riveting. This simple process and its underlying principle was akin to upsetting. By 1900, factory-made rivets were available in any sizable town; nevertheless, out of habit, and probably because it was both economical and convenient, many blacksmiths went on making their own. The rivet—nothing more than a length of round iron bar—was heated and inserted in holes punched ahead of time. By hammering first one hot end, then the other, two lumps of iron were created from which the finished heads were formed. At the same time, the shaft of the rivet inside the joint swelled into tight contact with the surrounding metal. A few deft strokes of the ball peen hammer rounded both heads neatly. Riveting was not nearly as strong as welding, but it was adequate in many places and it was a great deal faster. It provided a practical way of attaching blades to garden tools, and it was used in the making of shears, blacksmith tongs, and other tools with moveable arms. But the careful smith put a slip of heavy wrapping paper between the two arms before heading the rivet, to allow a bit of clearance so the arms would move.

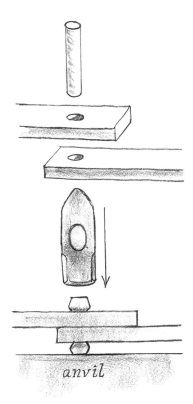

anvil

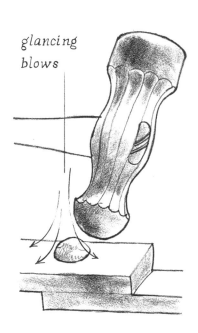

glancing blows

Tempering. Crudely defined, tempering of a tool was a two-stage process: first hardening it by heating and rapid quenching, and then reheating it and allowing some of the heat to draw off before again quenching it at a specified point in its cooling, to achieve a particular degree of hardness.

wagon tongue

Starting with a blank of unhardened steel, the blacksmith forged the tool to shape while the metal was in its annealed, softer state. Then the tool was bedded in a clean fire just far enough to bury the tip and a short distance beyond, where it was left to absorb heat gradually until it was a light cherry red. At that point it was suddenly quenched by plunging it into the water of the slack tub to the depth of the portion to be hardened, and rapidly swirled about. This agitation was necessary, particularly in quiet water, as steam generated so rapidly that vapor pockets formed on the metal, tending to retard the cooling. Rapid movement dissipated these bubbles, allowing more constant contact between the metal and the colder portions of the quench bath. When cool enough to be safely handled, the tool was taken out of the bath—now in a quite hard condition but at the same time much too brittle to be used without chipping or fracturing. In general, the more rapid the quench, the finer the internal structure of the metal, and the harder and more brittle it would be.

The second stage—drawing temper, or drawing color—involved re-heating the tool over the shank portion, well back from its working end, until a rainbow of color bands appeared on the tool's surface. At that moment, the blacksmith removed the tool from the fire and, in order to observe more accurately the colors, polished its surface using an abra-sive such as a piece of emery paper or an old brick. Viewed in the dim light of the shop, the color spectrum ranged from a bright yellow nearest the tool's tip, through pale yellow to straw, dark straw, purple, and blue. Each color and shade of color corresponded roughly to a hardness temperature. As this color band moved along the tool out toward the tip, the blacksmith watched its progress carefully, having calculated be-forehand the temper his tool required. When the desired color reached the end of the tool, he again thrust it into the slack tub.*

*Table 2 in the Appendix shows the relation of color to temperature for various types of tools.

Not infrequently, blacksmiths managed to combine both stages in a single heat, when they hardened and tempered by quenching only the working end of the tool, leaving most of the body and the shank relatively soft. The surface was then polished in the same way and the color band watched closely as the selected color moved toward the tool's end. At the critical moment, it was quenched.

If it is assumed that the blacksmith's stock of metal was limited to nothing but the wrought iron described earlier as "practically free of carbon," then any discussion of tempering would justifiably be out of place here. For while it had superior properties for forging and forge welding, as well as having a remarkable resistance to shock and to rusting, its low carbon content made it untemperable.

However, from numerous references in the literature to the knowledge gained from "accidental" steel making, it is probable that the blacksmith's supply of raw material included steels of a sort from which he was able to satisfactorily forge and temper—in his own way—at least some edge tools.

Blister steel and crucible steel were being manufactured on a commercial scale in Europe in the late 1800s. These were types of steel akin to the variety made either accidentally in the old forges or intentionally by pit-soaking, in which wrought iron was packed round with charcoal in clay containers and held under constant heat for a number of days. Under these conditions the iron absorbed from the charcoal sufficient amounts of carbon to become a steel.

According to the *Encyclopedia Britannica*, "Blister steel was, and still is, made by packing wrought iron bars in a long stone box full of charcoal, and heating the container for several days at a full red....But obviously this very indirect method of getting steel, bit by bit, was totally incapable of supplying the needs of the coming mechanical age."

Generally speaking, the nineteenth-century blacksmith did not have the advantages either of sophisticated equipment such as gas-fired blowpipes, muffle furnaces, and pyrometers, or of convenient access to the latest technical information from other parts of the world. He relied on experience acquired through trial and error, experimentation, and a critical eye.

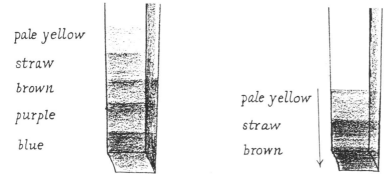

pale yellow
straw
brown
purple
blue

pale yellow
straw
brown

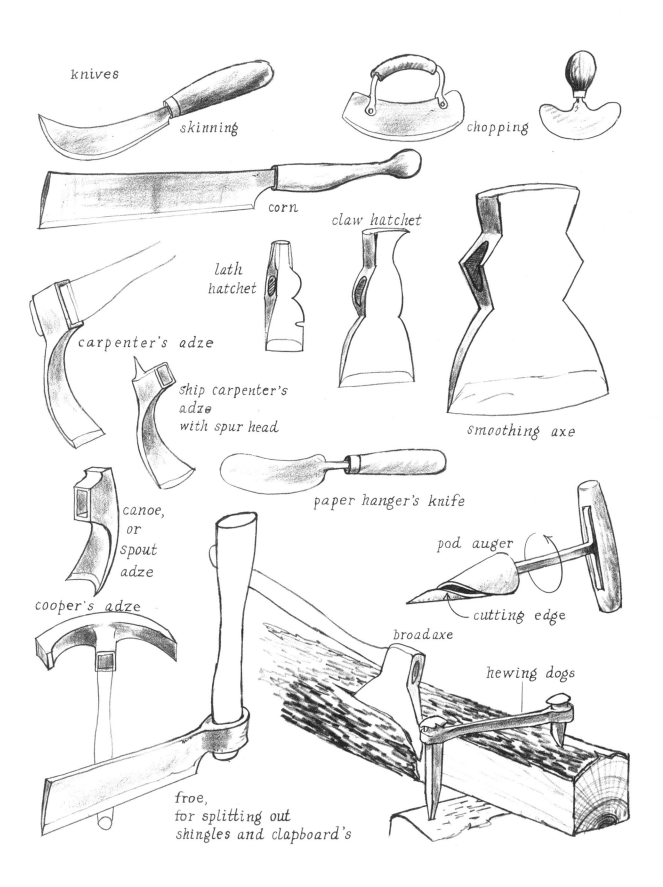

knives

skinning

chopping

corn

claw hatchet

lath hatchet

carpenter's adze

ship carpenter's adze with spur head

smoothing axe

paper hanger's knife

canoe, or spout adze

pod auger

cutting edge

cooper's adze

broadaxe

hewing dogs

froe, for splitting out shingles and clapboard's

Hardware and Harness

6

In this late-nineteenth-century period, which depended on horse power and was geared to horse-drawn vehicles, a large part of the New England blacksmith's work was connected with shoeing horses, making new wagon tires, and forging the countless odds and ends of metal parts and fittings used in the construction of sleds, sleighs, buggies and wagons, and a variety of horse-drawn farm implements. It was a society dominated by hand labor, performed with hand tools. The village population was made up mainly of farmers, millworkers, and tradesmen. Nearly all of them provided their own food, drink, and meat, tending a homestead garden, a small flock of hens, a hog or two, and occasionally holding a half-interest in a beef steer. The family cow grazed in the back pasture along with a driving horse or two that worked as well harnessed to a plow or hay wagon. Like his frugal fellow townsmen, the blacksmith butchered a hog for the winter, canned his fruits and vegetables, made apple butter and cider, and put down the extra eggs in waterglass against the time when the hens suspended work. If his wife's butter churn broke down, he could mend it in a few minutes. But he also mended everyone else's churn, as well as their shovels, spades, plows, axes, pitchforks, barn-door hinges, and garden hoes. Tools inevitably wore out or broke down, and they went to the smithy to be mended. They were never thrown away, for the blacksmith could usually manage to make an inexpensive repair. If the tool was beyond mending, he would make a reasonable copy, salvaging what iron remained and adding new metal to it by welding. When all was lost, when the tool was worn beyond any sort

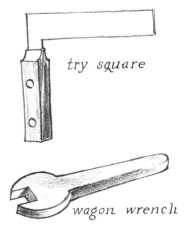

try square

wagon wrench

53

of fixing—and it didn't happen very often—then the blacksmith could allow something off the price of a brand-new tool, throwing the junk iron outside to be used sometime later. There was an unending demand for door hinges, latches, locks, and particularly for nails for building construction. The fireplace had to have andirons, a fire shovel, poker, and a pair of tongs, for wood supplied the only heat for cooking and warmth.

Winter was a time of change for the blacksmith, but it was not a period of long rest. The countryside was blanketed with snow; at times the roads were sheathed in ice and the fields swept by biting winds. For a people who were used to working outdoors, winter was a time with little to do but pitch hay to the animals and shovel paths from the kitchen door to the outbuildings. The life of the farmer revolved around

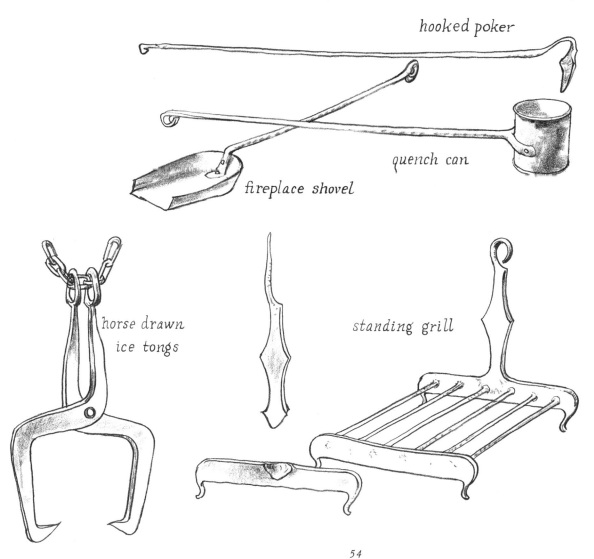

hooked poker

quench can

fireplace shovel

horse drawn ice tongs

standing grill

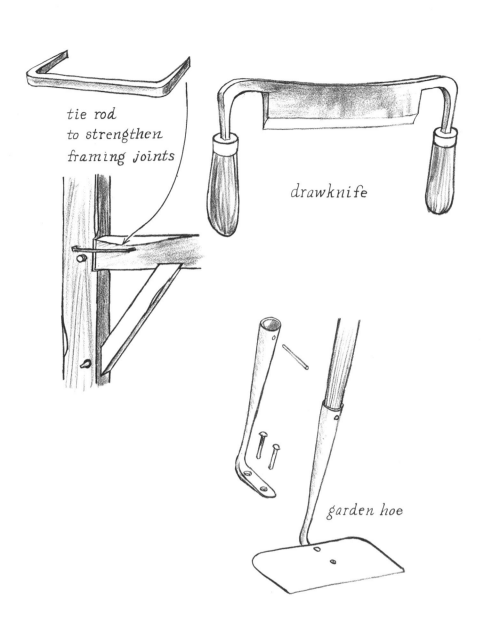

tie rod
to strengthen
framing joints

drawknife

garden hoe

heavy, barn door pintle

eye bolt

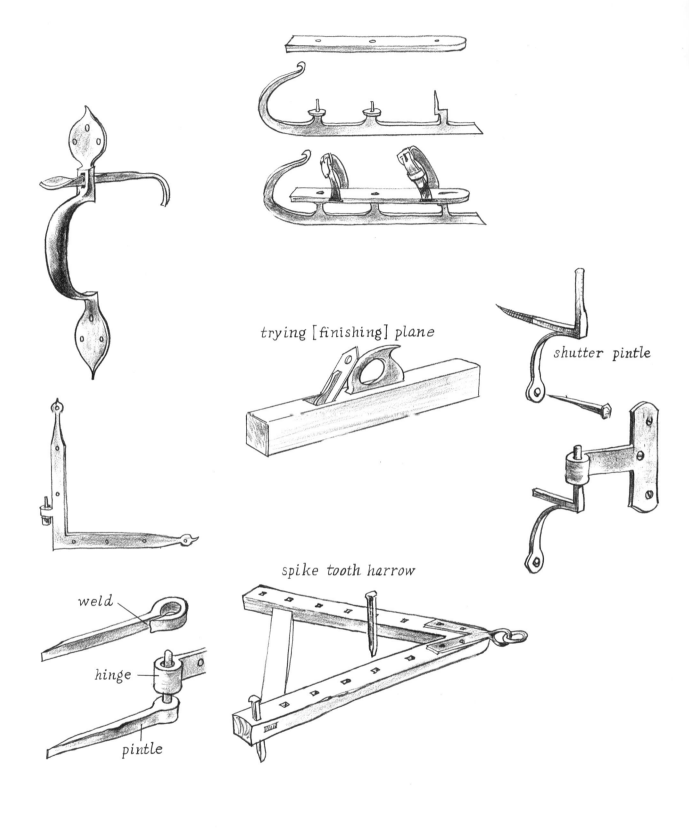

trying [finishing] plane

shutter pintle

spike tooth harrow

weld

hinge

pintle

the barn, the woodshed, the kitchen stove, and the big round table in the dining room where the farm magazines had been collecting, waiting to be read. Winter provided the farmer's only real leisure.

But for the blacksmith there were few long winter evenings when he could sit by the stove and study the almanac. He stood at his forge all day long and often late into the evening, mending the things the farmers had let go till after harvest time. As soon as the snow came, buggies and wagons were maneuvered into the back of the barn, and the sleighs and sleds were dragged out. If a buggy wheel wobbled on its way to winter storage, off it came, to be thrown on the log scoot for a trip to the blacksmith. Anything broken that lay about the shed, barn, or back room of the house was put in a box on the sled to go in for repairs on the same trip. Chains, axes, plowshares, grab hooks, a pair of broken shafts—the whole assortment went off to the blacksmith shop.

One of the routine seasonal activities that put a strain on the blacksmith's time was that of woodcutting. As every house in the village or

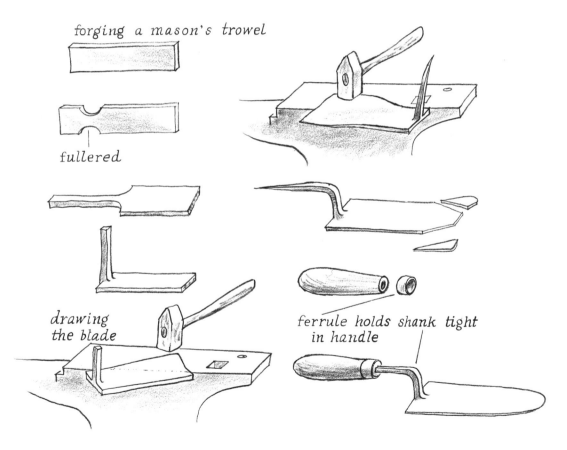

forging a mason's trowel

fullered

drawing the blade

ferrule holds shank tight in handle

57

on the farm was heated by wood, the coming of winter was the signal to "get out the wood." Farmers hitched their teams to the log scoots and commenced the long chore of hauling in next year's wood, load after load. It was a hard job at best, but the snow made the hauling a good deal easier. Besides, with the leaves off the trees a man could see around the woods better. To the blacksmith, woodcutting time meant more long days filled with the forging of new irons for sled runners, repairing chains, making grab hooks, and sharpening peavies that were used for rolling logs. Axes had to be refaced, crosscut saws sharpened, and the thick iron felling wedges dressed up clean and sharp.

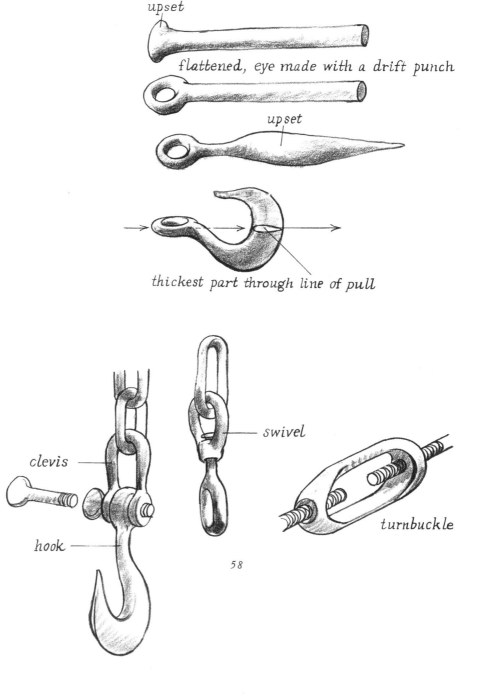

peavey —
for handling logs

upset

flattened, eye made with a drift punch

upset

thickest part through line of pull

clevis

swivel

hook

turnbuckle

58

And always there were horses to be shod. It was the practice to fit horses with winter shoes to give them better traction on ice. Special shoes with holes were nailed on and sharp lugs, or *caulks*, were fitted into the holes. As the mercury dropped and the frozen skin on the ponds thickened, ice-cutting time loomed ahead. More caulked horseshoes were needed, ice saws had to be sharpened, and ice axes made ready. About this time, hibernating farmers might decide it would be a good idea to have new butcher knives made and a supply of nails forged in order to be ready for spring building repairs. The blacksmith had to see to his own work too, somehow finding spare time between paying jobs to

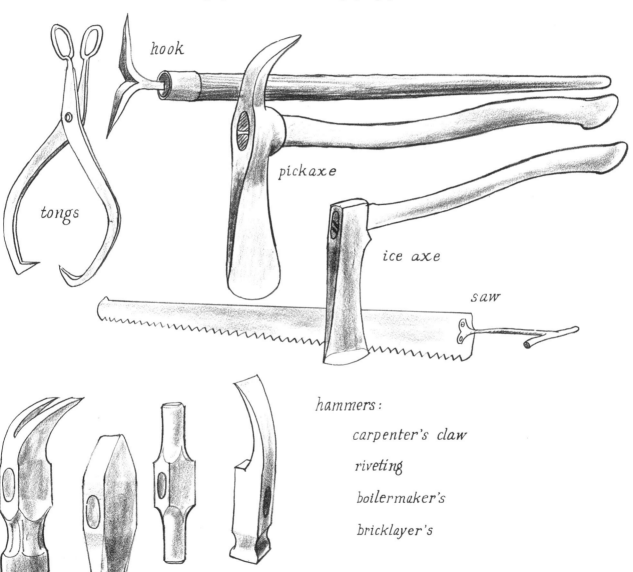

hook

pickaxe

tongs

ice axe

saw

hammers:

    carpenter's claw

    riveting

    boilermaker's

    bricklayer's

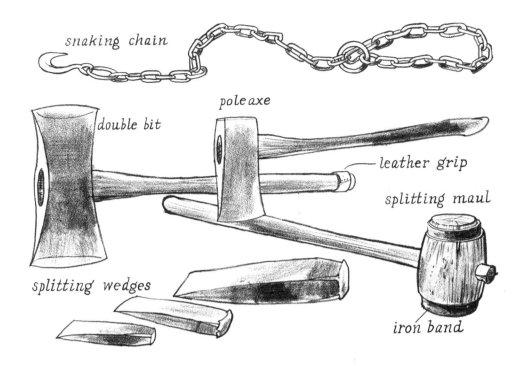

snaking chain

double bit

pole axe

leather grip

splitting maul

splitting wedges

iron band

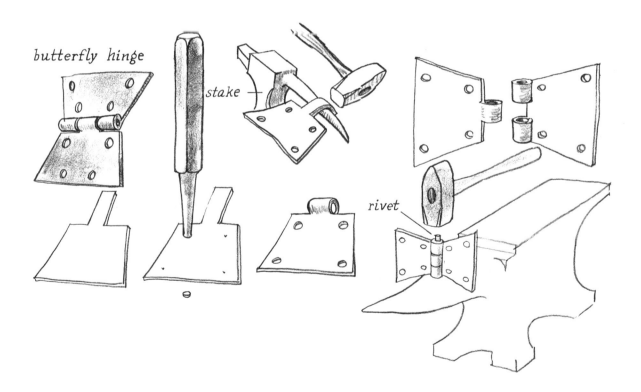

butterfly hinge

stake

rivet

make new swages, fit new handles into his sledges and hammers, or shore up a sagging floor beam with a chunk of locust.

On some warm, sunny day in mid-February the sugar maples were likely to begin running sap, and that meant sugaring time. Then all other work was abandoned; men stayed home from the mill and a general, undeclared holiday was observed. All it meant to the blacksmith, though, was more work: chains to be repaired, sled runners to be ironed, and of course more horses to be shod. At the end of a job the smith might very likely swap his labor for a few gallons of maple syrup, provided he hadn't used any new iron. If he had, then he collected cash for the iron; he could afford to swap his time but not iron.

On the heels of sugaring came spring plowing. The land had to be fitted for planting, which meant getting the harrows and cultivators in shape. The farmers who had put off this repair work stood in line at the smithy with their plowshares, spike harrows, broken corn planters and hand tools. An average plowshare weighed from nine to twelve pounds, and it was made of malleable chilled steel—an expensive item. With iron at a premium price, some way was usually found to make new plowshares out of old ones. A share that was only slightly worn could be heated cherry red and drawn out to its former size. This stretching—done with a hammer—made the share thinner, but at least it put some extra mileage into the old plow. Even a badly worn share that would no longer turn a furrow could be restored by welding an extra piece of iron to its point, then reshaping it to its original pattern. Throwing an old plowshare away and having a completely new one made was rarely even considered.

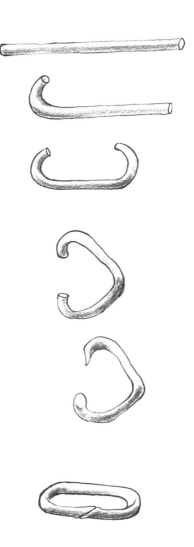

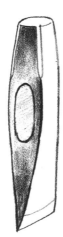

splitting axe

long pieces of chain made up from small sections of three or four links

61

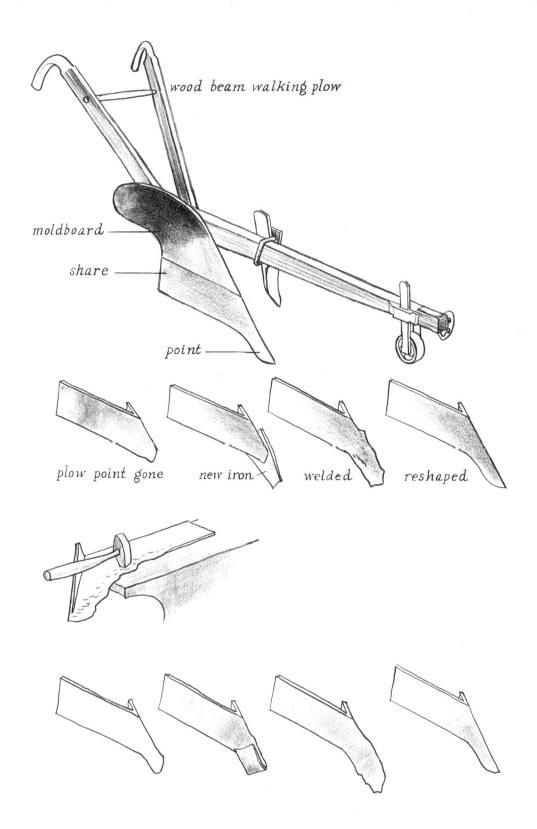

wood beam walking plow

moldboard

share

point

plow point gone   new iron   welded   reshaped

trowels:

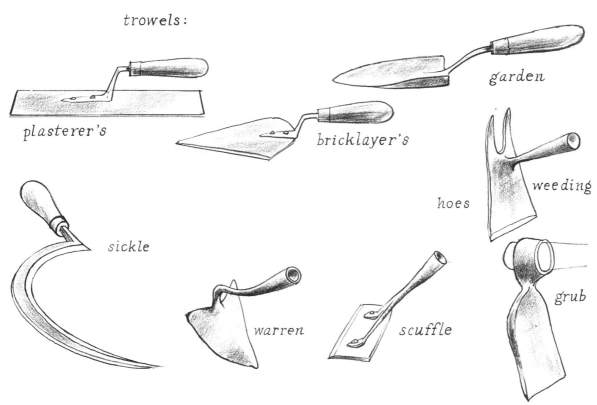

plasterer's

garden

bricklayer's

hoes

weeding

sickle

warren

scuffle

grub

When haying time came, the blacksmith was besieged by another on-rush of urgent work. One farmer needed some new teeth put into his horse rake; another brought in a mower bar that had struck a rock, twisting out of shape. As the hot, dry days of summer came on, wagon wheels began to work loose in the joints, and they were carried to the smithy to be rebuilt. Like the faces of the men who owned the wagons, each wheel had its own set look. The blacksmith didn't have to put tags on things; he simply stood the work along the wall and finished each piece as it came.

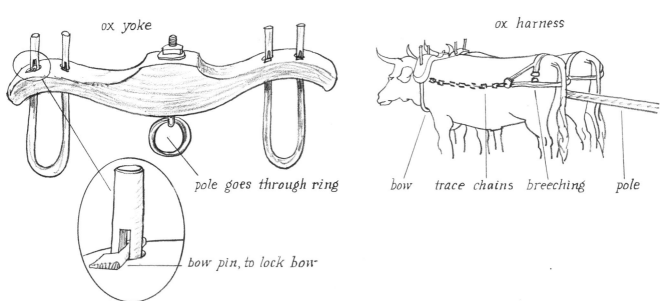

ox yoke

ox harness

pole goes through ring

bow pin, to lock bow

bow   trace chains   breeching   pole

In the fall the smith was occupied with work on butchering tools—sticking knives, bell scrapers, chain hoists, and all the rest. Each season brought its own work, and unless he worked long hours the blacksmith fell behind. Soon snow would fly again and a new cycle would be under way: woodcutting, ice cutting, sugaring, spring plowing, haying, harvesting—on and on it went.

cleaver

bell scraper

Throughout the entire year another steady flow of work demanded the blacksmith's attention. Each horse and each team had its own carefully fitted set of harness. This intricate network of leather straps, loops, and pads was of course held together with iron fittings—rivets, rings, lengths of small chain, bolts, clips, and hooks. And like every other article connected with the life of the times, these indispensable iron bits were forever breaking and wearing out. New sets of harness came from the harness maker in a large town, or from the mail-order house. Though the smith could have, he seldom did start from scratch to make a whole set of harness. But the mail-order house was far away, usually in some such place as Ohio, and the nearest harness maker was often two or three counties distant; so this additional repair and replacement work fell to the blacksmith. He was not a trained harness man—just an ingenious workman. He turned the iron work nicely, but his leather work—that was something else again. It might come out a bit clumsy, a little thick, and a trifle awkward. Yet when he finished mending a piece of harness it stayed mended; next time it would break in a new spot. For this work the blacksmith had special awls, a leather punch for making holes, knives for paring down the edges of leather, and a few heavy needles for patching tears in horse collars.

On the rare occasions when work was slack—and those must have been rare indeed—the blacksmith might work on a piece of his own ironwork. The very few remaining examples of the blacksmith's ornamental iron skill bear no signature to indicate who made them—such things as boot scrapers and fancy door latches, designed at the anvil

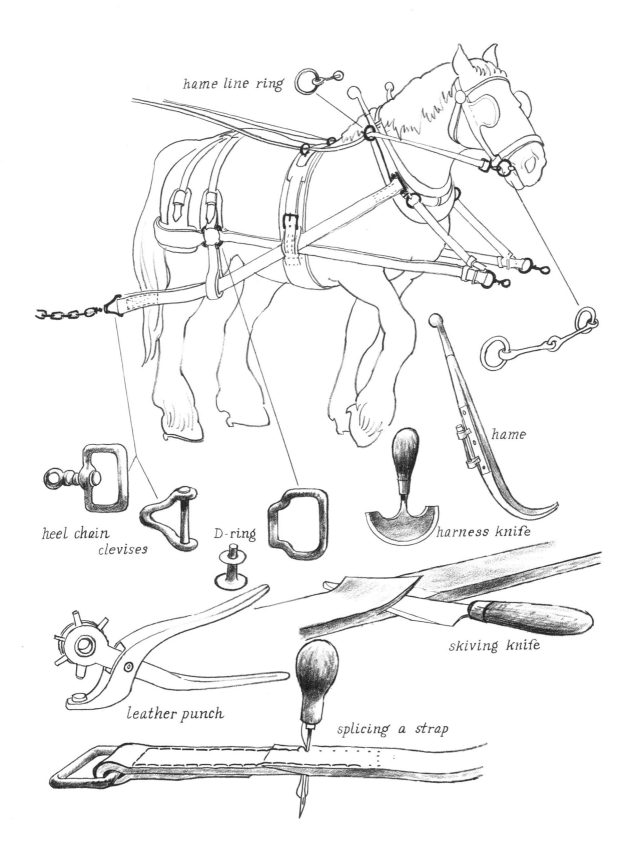

hame line ring

hame

heel chain clevises

D-ring

harness knife

skiving knife

leather punch

splicing a strap

and forged into gracefully curved works of art. Working in odd moments, the smith might spend eight or nine months completing such a luxury article, but when finished it pleased his wife and would outlast the house and everyone in it.

In the 1920s the decaying ruins of dozens of abandoned New England farms revealed the vestiges of the anvil age. There were the hinges and door latches, the iron coat hooks, the fireplace cranes, and the iron kettles—incongruously overgrown with brambles and milkweed, but as serviceable as the day they cooled at the forge. The

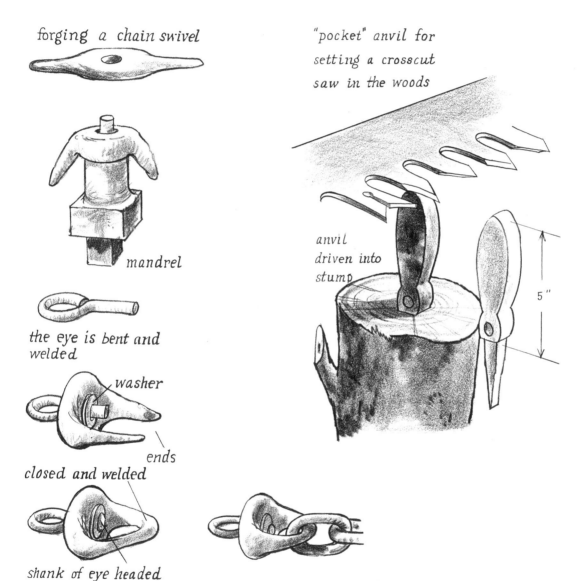

forging a chain swivel

mandrel

the eye is bent and welded

washer

ends

closed and welded

shank of eye headed

"pocket" anvil for setting a crosscut saw in the woods

anvil driven into stump

5"

66

barns and outbuildings still contained wagons, buggies, chains, and the ironwork of a past era. As the buildings caved into the cellar holes, collectors removed and carried away everything that could be taken. Even the old square-cut nails and spikes found their way to the antique shops. Most of the horseshoes, though, had long since been picked up and nailed to doorposts all over the land—most of them with the open end up to "keep in the good luck," only a few with the open end down to "pour forth luck onto the forge," which is how the blacksmith would have had it.

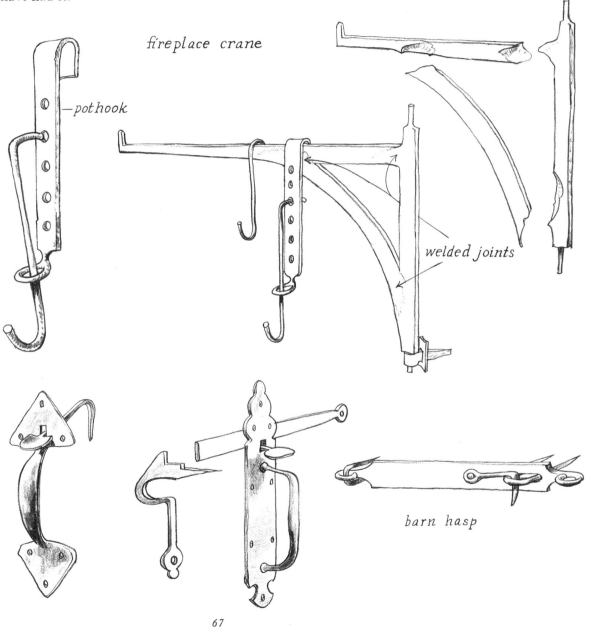

fireplace crane

—pothook

welded joints

barn hasp

67

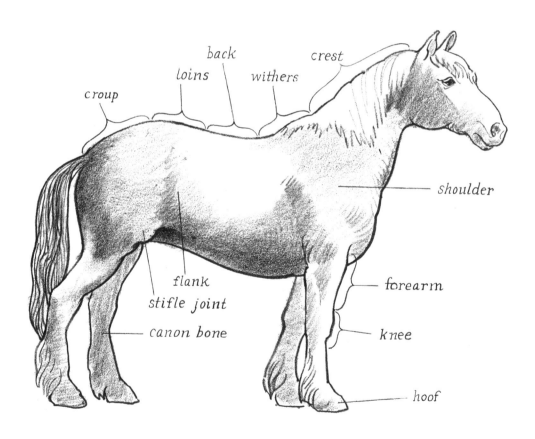

back

loins

withers

crest

croup

shoulder

flank

stifle joint

forearm

canon bone

knee

hoof

Shoeing a Horse

7

The most obvious reason for shoeing a horse was to prevent his feet from wearing out. The wild horse was seldom beset with foot troubles because he roamed grass-sodded ground—a more or less resilient surface. The trouble started when horses were put into harness and made to pound along hard-packed dirt roads or cobblestone highways, carrying or hauling loads that were equal to or greater than their own weight. Not only did their hoofs wear down but other, more serious troubles developed. The jarring impact on hard surfaces caused trouble in horses' joints and in the bony structure of their feet and legs, as well as in their nervous and circulatory systems. As the old Cockney verse has it,

> It ain't the 'unting wot 'urts the 'orse's 'oof;
> It's the steady 'ammer, 'ammer, 'ammer on the 'ard 'ighway.

Ancient armies may have moved on their stomachs, but it was the horse that hauled the impedimenta of war and carried soldiers into battle, more often than not returning with sore feet and stiff knees. The pack horses of Alexander the Great's armies are said to have suffered cruelly during the land marches through Asia; great numbers of them were abandoned when they went lame. When the Greeks, and later the Romans, saw their transport beasts breaking down because of sore feet, they sought ways to protect the horses' hoofs with padding. They tried all sorts of materials—leather, broom corn. reeds and other vegetable fibers. These soft shoes were a help but they wore out too quickly, and

iron hipposandal:
54-68 A.D.

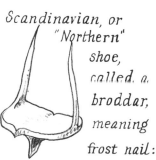

Scandinavian, or
"Northern"
shoe,
called a
broddar,
meaning
frost nail:
about 8th or 9th Cent.

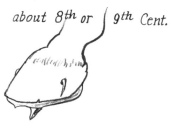

some of them produced sores from the chafing of the leather thongs and other straps used to bind them to the horse's feet. In Aristotle's time, camels used as military baggage carriers were often shod with a kind of sock bound to their feet. Just when the first iron shoes were used is not at all clear, although it must have been very near the time of Christ, for excavations in Germany, France, and England—wherever the Romans had been—have turned up variations of the horseshoe as we know it. They were called hipposandals (from the Greek *hippos*, a horse) and were crescent-shaped iron sandals laced to the horse's feet with leather straps. One excavation in France, on the site of Caesar's siege of Alesia (52 B.C.), yielded many small iron horseshoes, with their iron T-shaped nails still intact, indicating that they were nailed on in the same way that shoes are today. A great many of these ancient shoes had evidently been forged and then punched with holes, judging by the swelling of iron around each hole. The nails were not cut off after setting the shoe; they were simply bent down and hammered flat against the outside of the hoof.

In Roman times, the man who worried about horses' feet and was concerned about the kind of stabling they had was the *ferrarius*. Because he already knew the ironworking trade, he quite naturally took on the job of shoeing horses when iron shoes replaced those made of other materials. As he devised shoes to correct faults and remedy foot ailments, the term began to take on the additional meaning of veterinary. When the French turned the word into *ferrier*, it retained its veterinary connotation; and an obsolete meaning of our own word *farrier* is a veterinary, especially one who treats horses. Properly speaking, then, the term that specifically applies to a shoer of horses is farrier and not blacksmith.

Although horses still go lame, and some farriers may not have the anatomical knowledge of a veterinary, the crescent horseshoe has persisted; it is still being used today, with hardly any variation in its design or in the design of the horsenail. The iron shoe did eliminate the wearing down of hoofs, but it did not overcome the orthopedic difficulties that often result from its use. The New England blacksmith worked with these problems, made special shoes, wedged them, or devised clamps to hold a cracked hoof together. But when all was said and done, shoeing a horse was not quite as simple as bolting irons to the runners of a sled.

Horses were shod for reasons other than just protecting the hoofs. When the road was a sheet of ice, a horse encumbered by a webbing of leather harness and dragging a sled behind him often lost his natural balance and fell. Special winter shoes were therefore made which had sharp studs attached to them to give the animal a firm footing on ice. And as the farrier's art and knowledge grew, the many different kinds of weighted, wedged, and built-up shoes that were produced made some inroads on the other problems related to anatomy. Whether or not the blacksmith was a qualified veterinary, he absorbed enough of the rudi-

ments of horse anatomy to enable him to set shoes with a fair degree of
success.

A horse's leg is an elaborate mechanism with many moving parts that hinge, rotate, and bend as the foot strikes the ground.* In order to bear the animal's weight when hauling or running, this complex articulation of bone, cartilage, and hoof needs the freedom to flex, bend, and spread: every part of the intricate assembly has to work if the shock of impact on the ground is to be taken up normally. The leg terminates in an elastic, spongy pad called the *frog,* with hoof, or horny shield, around it. The frog and the hoof together take the first shock when the foot strikes the ground, so it is clear that the length relation of the hoof to the frog will affect how much of this severe impact is transferred to the leg bone above. Pare the hoof too low and all the shock is shifted to the frog. Just as much jarring is created by letting the hoof grow too long, for then the frog becomes useless and the hoof is likely to crack or split. At the moment of impact, the hoof spreads sideways, buffering the blow still more. In the wild state, the horse's hoofs grew and replaced themselves, and as the horse clambered over rocky terrain they wore down naturally into the proper relation to the frog.

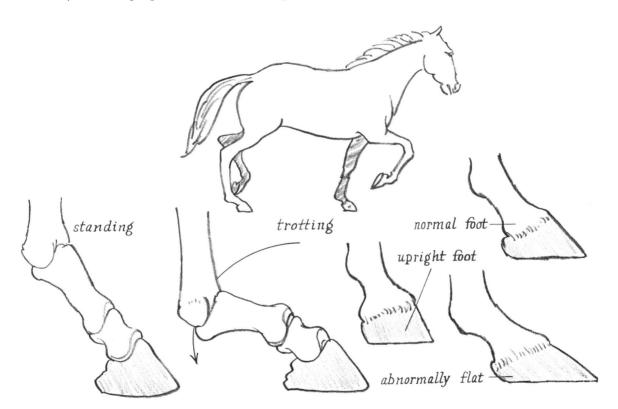

standing   trotting   normal foot

upright foot

abnormally flat

* See Table 1 in the Appendix for a study on hoof expansion.

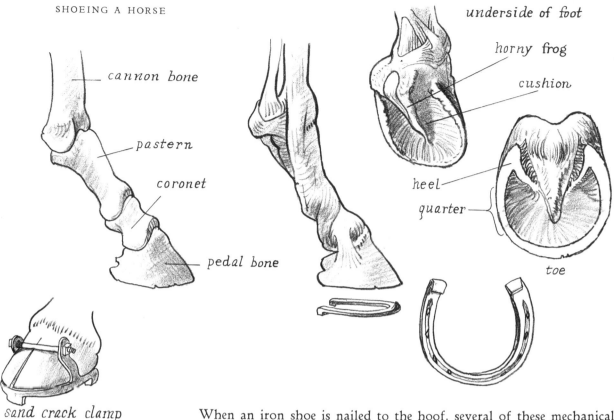

underside of foot

cannon bone

pastern

coronet

pedal bone

horny frog

cushion

heel

quarter

toe

sand crack clamp

quarter crack

clamp

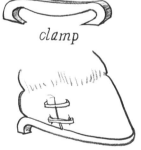

When an iron shoe is nailed to the hoof, several of these mechanical actions are restricted: the hoof cannot spread, and unless the exact thickness of the horseshoe is accounted for when paring the hoof, the frog may stay completely clear of the ground. Furthermore, with a metal plate between the hoof and the ground, every step is that much more hard-hitting. Unhappily for the horse, it was not until the late 1800s that the farrier's art recognized the horse's foot as a living organism requiring a good deal of anatomical knowledge to properly shoe it.

When a horse was brought in, the blacksmith first looked him over carefully. While a boy held the horse's halter, the smith walked around the animal, checking the condition of his feet, and the old shoes. Any hoof cracks? How much hoof needs to be pared off? Will new shoes be needed, or is there enough wear left in the old ones to justify resetting them? How does the animal stand? Anything peculiar about his walk? The blacksmith might then have the boy lead the horse outside and walk and trot him up and down the yard, the better to see any flaws in his gait. A horse whose hind feet caught up with and tripped his front feet was said to "click." When either the front or hind feet struck the opposing ones in trotting, he was said to "interfere." Striking the front foot with the hind one on the same side was called "forging." Special shoes could be made to help reduce these faults. For example, extra iron

could be welded to one side of the shoe to throw the horse's foot to
one side or the other. The blacksmith used small iron clips and clamp
shoes to hold badly cracked hoofs together. And by building up one or
the other side of a horseshoe with extra metal, the stance of a horse's
foot could be improved.

Now to take off the old shoes. The smith always talked to the horse,
especially a new one, to put him at ease. After a few gentle slaps on the

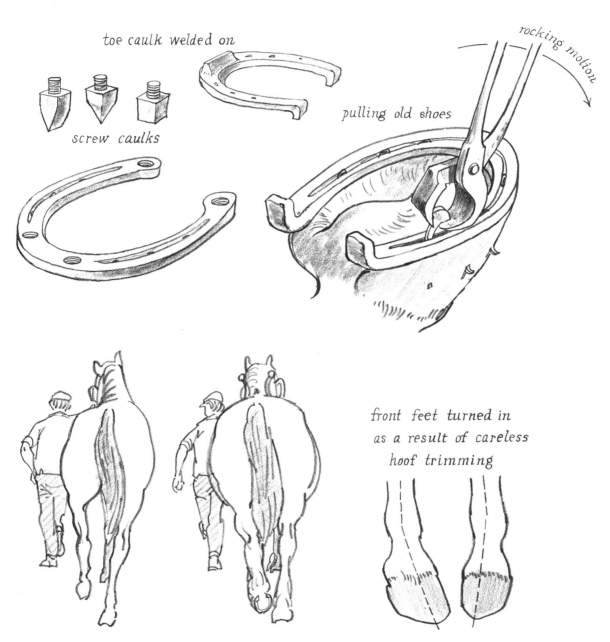

toe caulk welded on

screw caulks

pulling old shoes

rocking motion

front feet turned in
as a result of careless
hoof trimming

horse's shoulder, the smith would pick up a front foot and cradle it in his lap. With the buffer iron and hammer he bent the clinches out, then worked the shoe loose, pulling the old nails with his pincers. He started with the heel of the shoe, working the nails loose a little at a time so as not to damage the hoof wall. Then he tossed the shoe aside and cleaned out the sole of the foot, scraping all the caked mud, dirt, and gravel from around the frog.

The hind foot was picked up in much the same way, except that the smith was a bit more cautious. A horse doesn't usually mind having his front feet worked on because he can see what is going on. But when the smith gets to the hind feet he is out of the horse's range of vision. This makes some horses a bit touchy. So the blacksmith, still talking, would place his hand on the horse's rump, then slide it down the animal's leg until it reached the thick hair of the fetlock. This gave the smith something to take hold of. As he picked up the foot, the blacksmith took a step away from the horse's rear end and swung his knee under the horse, leaving the upturned hoof in his lap. In this position, even if the horse kicked, the smith could step out of the way and not be sent sprawling. Most horses, whenever one of their feet was picked up, instinctively shifted their weight to the other three. There were some wise

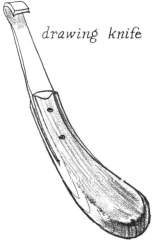

drawing knife

piece of mower section welded into caulk

nail cap

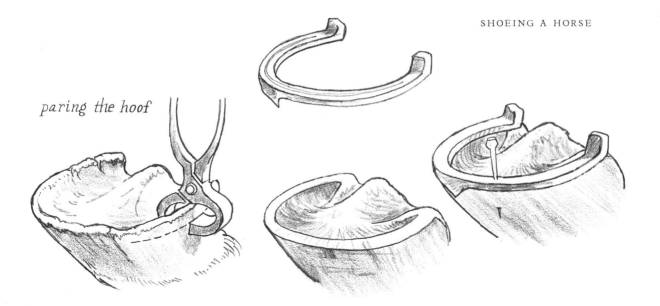

paring the hoof

old nags, however, that tried to make the blacksmith hold them up, a state of affairs that even the mightiest man could not stand for long.

When he had pulled all the shoes, the blacksmith next made the round of all four feet again, paring each hoof down to take off the dead growth. This he generally did with the short-blade hoof knife that he also used to clean out the sole. But if very much paring was called for, he used a pair of nippers. The blunt jaw was set against the outside of the hoof so that the sharp, cutting jaw would cut *away* from the inside of the foot. The smith trimmed clear round the hoof, a short section at a time, then leveled up the foot with a big flat rasp. If the slope of the hoof was too long, he could true it up by cutting off more of it at the toe. All this business required good judgment, since the comfort of the horse, as well as his efficiency at work, depended on well-trimmed feet. The shape of the hoof was the main thing; the iron shoe merely protected it from wearing down. An error in judgment at this point might mean waiting till the next shoeing—perhaps three months later when the hoof had grown out enough to need a new shoeing job—before the work could be corrected. As the smith finished each foot, the horse tested it on the floor while the blacksmith watched.

The time came when the smith could buy horseshoes ready-made, carting them from the railroad depot in lots of fifteen or twenty kegs. But until then, the blacksmith cut and forged all his own horseshoes from lengths of grooved shoe rod. Although he knew his old customers well enough to measure by eye the iron he would need, the smith's rule was to cut a length of iron about equal to twice the width of the horse's foot at its widest part, twice the thickness of the hoof wall, and the same width as the thickness of the hoof where it touched the ground.

All four shoes were forged and shaped before being nailed on. The smith generally made them up in pairs, working the front ones together, then making the hind shoes. The length of shoe iron was heated and then bent into a wide, open curve something like that of a boomerang. After another heating, the curve was closed by hammering over the horn of the anvil, and the two ends were brought closer together at the heel. Then the smith might take the shoe to the horse and lay it on his foot to see what further shaping was needed.

Then the shoe was ready for finishing. The blacksmith first forged a turned-up clip, called a "cat's ear," on the front part of the shoe. This

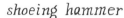

shoeing hammer

finished shoe

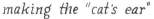

grooved shoe iron

nail holes punched

making the "cat's ear"

protected the toe of the hoof and kept the shoe from shucking. The front part of the shoe was heated and laid flat on the anvil, with the hot part projecting over the edge. A smart blow bent the cat's ear, and the sharp edge was smoothed off with a few light taps of the hammer. This was known as "toeing a shoe." The heel of the shoe was then heated and turned down into blunt caulks. If toe caulks were also wanted, short lugs were then welded onto the undersurface of the front of the shoe, and it was ready for punching.

Nail holes were punched in two stages, the first being done with a blunt punch simply to mark the location of the holes. These first punch marks were made on the heated horseshoe as it lay flat on the anvil with the inside of the shoe up. For the final punching, the shoe was turned over, and the hole driven through with a *pritchel*—a rectangular punch with a shank a little smaller than the neck of a horseshoe nail. This left a neat, tapered hole that would tightly grip the softer metal of the nail as it was driven home. Eight holes were punched in each shoe—six in

76

the case of a pony shoe. The completed shoe was finally hammered flat
to take out any unevenness left by the forging.

The horseshoes were fitted hot. This didn't hurt the horse in the least; the hoof is just as insensitive as a fingernail. The purpose of hot-fitting was to burn the hoof to conform to every irregularity of the iron, so that hoof and shoe would have complete contact at every point. A shoe fitted in this way stayed on longer because there was little chance it could begin to work loose.

When all four shoes were made, they were hung over the horn of the anvil to cool, and the smith dragged his box of farrier's tools close to the horse.

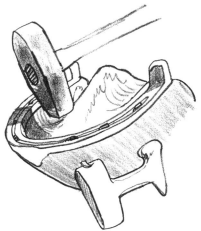

tightening a nail with the buffer

The horseshoe nail was made of soft metal, tapered down to a needle-sharp point. It had to be started into the hoof at just the right angle, aimed to enter the hoof wall and curve outward as it was driven home. The point had to come out through the wall of the hoof neither too high nor too low, about one and a half to two inches above the sole. If the nail went in too straight it was likely to strike the quick—the sensitive part of the horn. The blacksmith could tell by the sound of the nail under his hammer blows if it was going right. If not, the nail was pulled at once and another was started. The used nail was thrown away. As soon as the tip of the nail came through, the smith snagged it with the claws of his hammer, gave it a twist to break off the tip, and clinched down the ragged end. Another method of nailing a shoe was to bend the points over, then go round the shoe with the hammer and clinch block, tightening all the nail heads *before* clinching. In any event, the nail ends were always clinched so that no sharp ends were left.

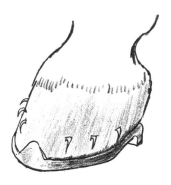

As a final bit of finishing, the edges of the newly shod feet were carefully rasped smooth just where the hoof met the shoe. The blacksmith was careful not to rasp the sides of the hoof, however, because it is protected by a natural varnish that conserves its moisture. Dry hoofs tend to crack easily, and dirt that works its way into a spreading crack leads to serious trouble.

The blacksmith shod all kinds of horses—little ones, big ones, mean ones, crafty ones. The gentle older animals were easy. They had been to the blacksmith shop many times, and they knew the smith well. And he knew them. These seasoned farm horses would stand as still as a post; a few even dozed while the blacksmith worked. But new horses had to be given special treatment. Neither the smith nor the horse knew exactly what to expect of each other. The horse was suspicious, the blacksmith cautious. A common trick in shoeing a newcomer or a skittish colt was to have an older horse come along as a companion. The two were then tied side by side and the work went on with far less trouble.

When the blacksmith had to work with an especially balky or mean horse, he resorted to special contrivances, all of them meant to restrain rather than pacify. Even at that, these devices had to be used in a quiet way, or the horse might get panicky. Only an absolutely pigheaded blacksmith would run the risk of clouting an animal for bad behavior. Antagonizing a horse only defeated the smith's purpose, for he knew quite well that the same animal would be back for his next set of shoes. The blacksmith and his helpers did well, therefore, to try for good relations on the first encounter.

For a horse that simply would not stand, the blacksmith had what was called a *twitch*—a short stick with a loop of rope knotted through a hole in one end. The loop was slipped over the horse's upper lip and nostrils, and with a twist of the wrist the smith could partially shut off the animal's wind—a crude but effective persuader. A horse that was a "kicker" could be made to restrain himself by lashing him up in a rope tied to his tail and looped around one of his hind feet. The loose end of

twitch

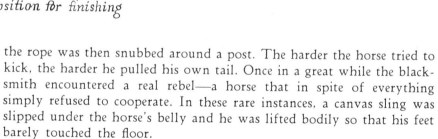

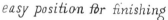

easy position for finishing

the rope was then snubbed around a post. The harder the horse tried to kick, the harder he pulled his own tail. Once in a great while the blacksmith encountered a real rebel—a horse that in spite of everything simply refused to cooperate. In these rare instances, a canvas sling was slipped under the horse's belly and he was lifted bodily so that his feet barely touched the floor.

However brutal these methods may seem, they were designed to accomplish just one thing—to get the horse shod quickly with as little damage as possible to man and beast. After the smith had worked a number of years with horses of all sizes and temperaments, he acquired as part of his skill an anvil manner diplomatic enough to reassure all but the meanest renegade. He had three personalities to worry about: his own, the horse's, and the owner's. If he satisfied all three, he would have a lifelong customer, and might even look for a barrel of cider every fall to see him through the winter.

Farmers who still used oxen were never very keen about bringing them in for shoeing, declaring that it was harder on the beasts than a week's work. The ox was very heavy, and not at all skillful at balancing on three legs. Almost invariably, therefore, the smith had to use the big canvas sling rigged to a windlass. The ox was lifted nearly off his feet, and the foot being shod was buckled to a padded foot rest so the work could proceed in peace. The shoes were, of course, made in two sections —one for each side of the ox's cloven hoofs—and the iron was somewhat thinner than that used for a horseshoe. Because the wall of an ox's hoof is not as thick as that of a horse, smaller nails and more of them were used to attach the shoes. Shoeing an ox must have been a trying, long-drawn-out affair, which may have been why the job brought a bigger

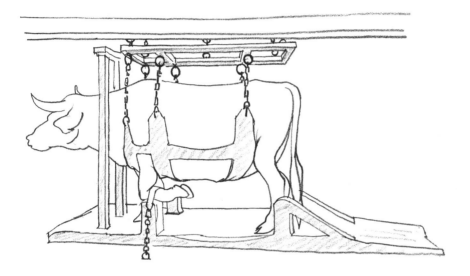

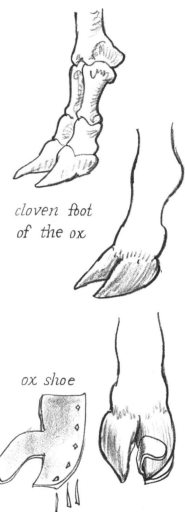

cloven foot of the ox

ox shoe

fee. At such times the blacksmith must have longed to be working with the kind of well-mannered pony that lifts his own foot off the floor the minute he feels a hand on him.

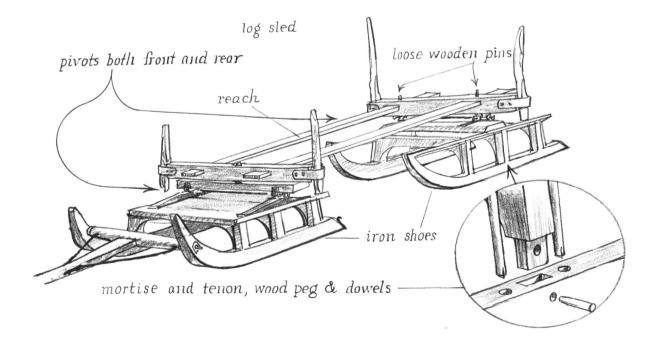

log sled

pivots both front and rear

loose wooden pins

reach

iron shoes

mortise and tenon, wood peg & dowels

Wagons, Buggies, and Sleds 8

Nearly every farm had a machine shed where its rolling stock was kept under cover from the weather. In one end of this long, rambling building —commonly attached to the back end of the house—stood the buggy. Mounted on thin springs and drawn by a high-stepping mare, this fragile-looking vehicle took the family to town for groceries, to the Saturday night kitchen dances, to church on Sunday, sedately to funerals, and even down through the back pasture with a load of fence posts. Backed into the cool shade of the shed, the idle buggy was also a beautiful place where the children played.

Alongside the buggy stood the spring wagon. Fitted with a pole and drawn by a pair of driving horses, it was a sturdy wagon that could carry the whole family on a long trip, or haul supplies back from the railroad depot. Then there was a heavy, high-wheeled farm wagon with removable side-boards that carted manure to the fields, or could easily be converted to a hay wagon by setting in place the "hayrick" body. Some farms also had a four-wheeled dump cart, and a few sported two-wheel pony carts for the youngsters.

At the other end of the shed were stored the cold weather counterparts of these vehicles, for no wheel would turn on New England's snow-clogged roads. When the snow got deep, it was up to the road commissioner to order out his teams and big rollers to pack out a smooth, hard surface for runners to glide over. Most farms had a family runabout—a one-horse sleigh with a gracefully curved dashboard and slender iron-shod runners. The boxlike pung resembled a spring wagon on runners.

As the snow deepened, the set of log scoots was dragged out; it had an adjustable reach to extend its length. This "work wagon on runners" made many trips between farmyard and woods, hauling cordwood and saw logs.

Wagons, buggies, and sleds were factory-built. Carriage shops all over the eastern half of the country were producing vehicles patterned after early models designed by such carriage makers as Louis Downing, of Lexington, Massachusetts, and James Brewster, of New Haven, Connecticut. At first they were all handmade, but even in the 1850s some of the more enterprising shops were using crude mass-production methods. G. and D. Cook, of New Haven, for example, increased their daily output by these means from one carriage a day to one every hour—a day's total of ten. Their shop employed 300 men in 24 separate departments. By 1900, there were 800 carriage-building shops in the United States, the larger ones giving work to an average of 15 blacksmiths, 15 woodworkers, 5 trimmers, and 15 or 20 painters.

A typical carriage shop occupied four floors and a basement. The blacksmith shop, with four forges, each with its own chimney, took up the whole basement. On the ground floor above was the main office, the delivery room, and a receiving room. The second floor was given over to the lumber loft, where the various kinds of hardwood were stuck up on racks to dry. The carpentry shop was on the third floor, and on the top floor was the paint and varnish shop. Such a factory building cost in the neighborhood of $16,000, without the land it stood on.

Every vehicle with wheels, as well as sleds and sleighs, was fastened together with iron parts and fittings forged by hand at the anvil. A single wheel, the tire included, required some fourteen separate iron forgings to hold it together. The entire wagon, complete with tongue, eveners, singletrees, and side-boards, represented about 117 fittings, 84 carriage bolts, 50 or 60 wood screws, and 8 to 12 feet of chain.

Stevens Abbott, who became a partner of Downing's, made this brief tally of some of their 1854 statistics:

> We sent carriages into every state, territory, and province in North America except Delaware. We employed on the average of 190 men, delivered 625 carriages, and used 300,000 feet of lumber, 50 tons of Cumberland coal, and 6,500 bushels of charcoal. We cannot now name the exact amount of iron, but about 250 tons.*

Carriage making was a specialized trade, requiring its own array of tools, equipment, and skilled labor force. The process of selecting the proper woods, drying them, and then cutting, fitting, joining, and finishing the dozens of pieces that went into the body work was as com-

* From E. V. Mitchell, *The Horse and Buggy Age in New England.*

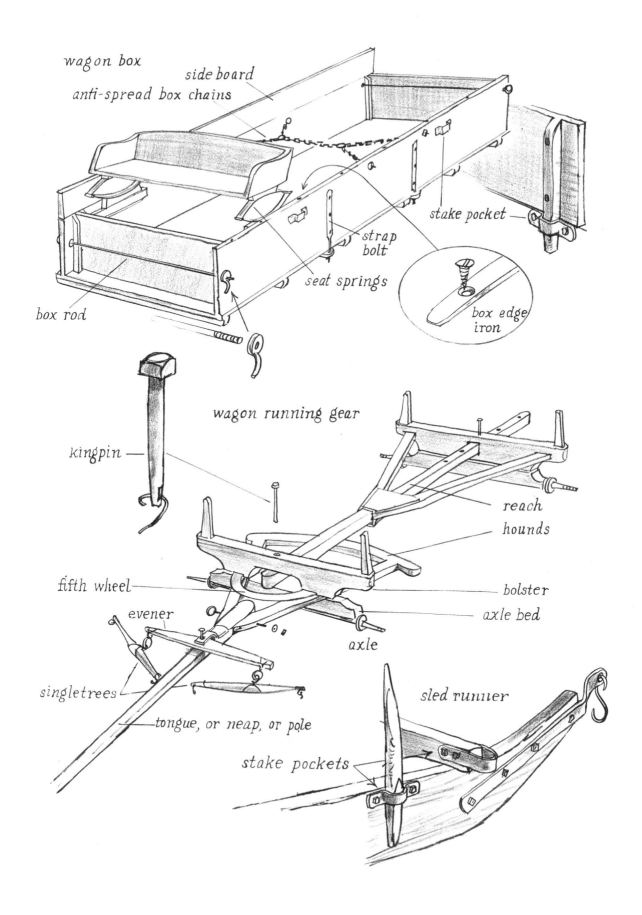

wagon box

side board

anti-spread box chains

stake pocket

strap bolt

seat springs

box rod

box edge iron

wagon running gear

kingpin

reach

hounds

fifth wheel

bolster

axle bed

evener

axle

singletrees

tongue, or neap, or pole

sled runner

stake pockets

mortise and tenon

*bevelled
shoulder*

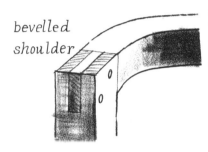

bare shoulder tenon

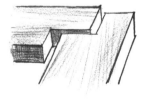

double tenon

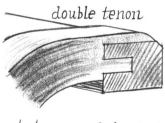

*run of the grain
for strongest
corner blocks*

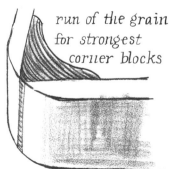

plex an industry in its own way as the blacksmith's. The village black-smith was set up to make repair parts, but in no sense of the word was he a carriage maker. Even those carriage shops that employed fifteen blacksmiths found, as early as 1800, that their smiths could not keep up with the production line. On the basis of Stevens Abbott's figures above, turning out 625 carriages a year meant that fifteen smiths were producing something like 73,125 separate iron parts, or an average of 4,875 each. Of some help was a new metal alloy beginning to attract attention; it was being used in the making of door latches, and carriage makers started using it for some of their hardware that didn't demand the strength of wrought iron. It could be cast in molds like cast iron, but it had more tensile strength than cast iron and was less brittle. Its use cut down on the amount of hand forging and thereby helped to increase output.

The finished wagons, buggies, and carriages were shipped to customers on railroad flatcars; once they found their way to a backwoods farm, the blacksmith in the village was the only man close by who knew the first thing about mending them. Old account books are peppered with scrawled entries that tell of his making new trace chains, ironing sled runners, or forging whiffletree hooks. And he made these replacement parts by the hundred—king pins, box rods, stake pockets, axles, and sets of matched nuts and bolts.

Carpentry wasn't the blacksmith's specialty either; yet he undertook to duplicate broken wooden members with his rudimentary set of wood-working tools. After he had fitted the parts together and bolted them tight, he could survey a piece of work fully as rugged as the original, if somewhat less artistic.

Wheelwrights and carriage makers chose woods that combined strength with the least weight and long life in the weather. Elm and black locust were favored for hubs, oak for spokes, and white ash for the felloes, or "fellies" as they were often called. The flexible, wiry ash was easily steam-bent to the curve of a wheel. The smith had little trouble duplicating felloes and spokes—the parts that were most likely to break. The countryside abounded in oak and ash, and with his simple foot-treadle lathe he could turn a spoke in short order.

The same craftsmanship was lavished on the frames, bodies, and boxes of farm vehicles. Strength and resistance to atmospheric change influenced the choice of woods for making the best bodies. The mortise and tenon joints were as tight in a sleigh body as those in the hub of the wheels. And they were made with the same precise measurements, careful chisel work, and snug-fitting pegs to hold the pieces together.*

The discerning blacksmith understood most of these techniques, though he seldom had the chance to use them himself. He knew how a

* In this same period, carpenters engaged in the framing of barns and covered bridges were equally intent on accuracy: marks for mortise and tenon joints were made with a sharp, thin penknife, not a pencil.

84

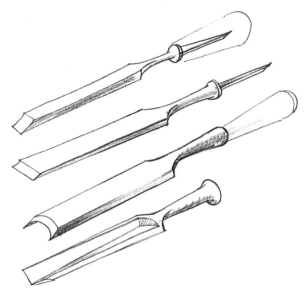

carriage maker's tools

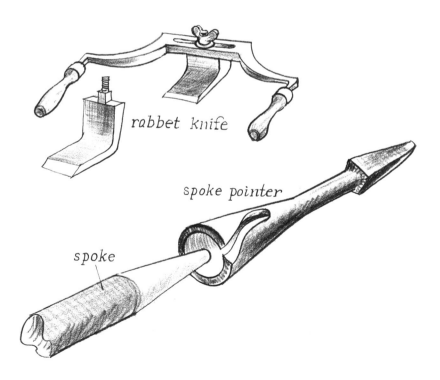

rabbet knife

spoke pointer

spoke

dovetail joint was made, but had to settle for a makeshift repair simply because he couldn't get at the joint to replace it exactly. Besides, his anvil acumen gave him license to use angle irons, plates, and other metal splints. The customer was interested in speed, strength, and economy, not in paying to have his buggy completely dismantled so that the repaired part would be identical to the original.

More than any other part of farm vehicles, the wheel caused the farmer the greatest anguish and the blacksmith the most work. The life expectancy of a wheel depended entirely on its being as tight as a drum. Each spoke had to fit the hub snugly, and each one of the felloes had to grip the end of the spoke like a vise. A good wheel, bound with an iron tire of just the right size, was as solid as a single disc of wood. But wheels took a terrible punishment. Wagons and buggies were driven through rough-plowed fields, over dirt roads full of potholes, through stone-bottomed brooks, and into rocky pastures, Left out in the open, their protective paint and varnish soon flaked off, leaving the bare wood exposed to the baking summer sun. Then the component parts of the wheel—all eighteen of them—shrank and warped. The spokes wobbled in the hub, the felloes worked loose, and the rim began to rattle. Worst of all, this death rattle soon shook out the tire bolts, the wheel lost its "dish," and finally collapsed in a heap of sticks.

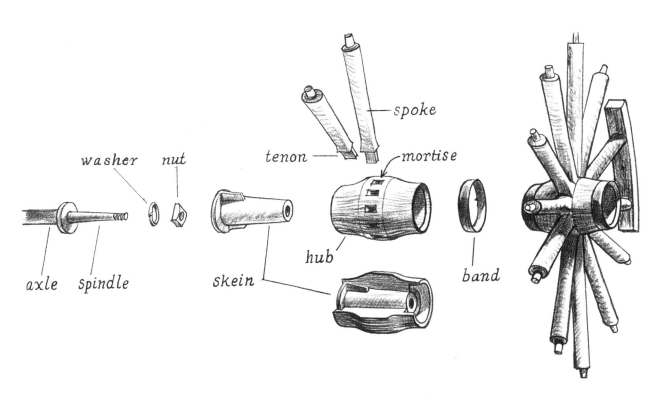

Until the time when Cyrus McCormick was getting ready to demonstrate his new reaping machine—1831—the iron tires of wagon wheels were not made in one continuous strip. Individual iron plates were bolted to the rim over the ends of the spokes, and similar plates were fastened to the sides of the rim where the felloes joined. But then an American blacksmith conceived the revolutionary idea—though he never got credit for it—of making one endless iron hoop to encircle the wheel. When this iron tire was heated red-hot it expanded; when it was driven hot onto the wheel and began to contract, the cooling iron winched all the parts of the wheel up as tight as a bowstring.

Wheels were ordinarily built with a concavity, or "dish." The perpendicular center line of the hub was not in line with the rim. The axle spindles were accordingly forged at an angle to match the dish of the wheel, thus putting the load on the perpendicular spoke. As the wheel turned, the natural thrust of the loaded wagon, pressing out against the hub and spokes, pushed against the dish. Of all the accidents that befell wheels, the most common and disastrous was the loss of dish. When the wheels began to look as though they were on the wrong side of the wagon, it was time to drive it gingerly to the blacksmith shop— empty.

There were several remedies for this condition. Which one was chosen

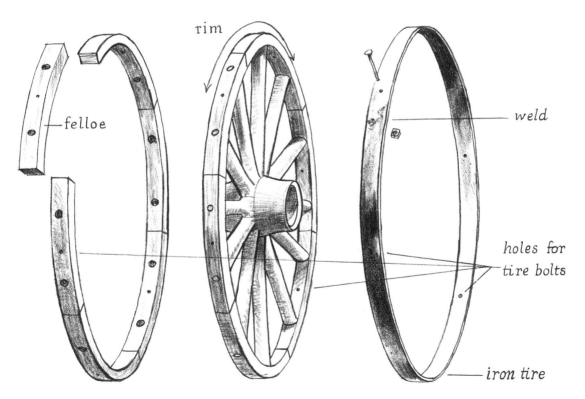

rim

felloe

weld

holes for
tire bolts

iron tire

depended on how long the wheel had been neglected. Caught with wobbly wheels in the middle of haying season, farmers generally tried the home cure first. This involved jacking up the wagon, pulling off the offending wheels, and rolling them down to the brook, where they would be left to soak overnight. The hub and spokes were pushed back into shape, and the wheel was shored up with stones to hold it in position. By morning the wood had swelled and tightened the joints—at least for long enough to get the last load of hay into the barn. Sooner or later, however, the whole wagon would have to go to the smithy.

A new wheel that had only recently dried out could be tightened with very little work. The smith first removed the tire by taking off the nuts and driving the bolts out through the rim. Usually the spokes would be found projecting beyond the outside of the rim, because the rim had shrunk. A quarter-inch was sawed off the spokes, the felloes were replaced, and the iron tire made ready for remounting. The blacksmith then put the tire in the fire and heated one part of it to a bright red. Next, with a good solid blow of the sledge hammer, he put a kink in the iron and clamped it into a shrinking tool set in the hardy hole of the anvil. A few more well-placed hammer blows flattened the kink, in effect easing the iron back into a shorter span.

When all four wheels had to be taken off the axles, the smith identified each one with pairs of punch marks to make sure each wheel would be returned to its rightful place. By making two single marks on the

clamp used for shrinking a tire

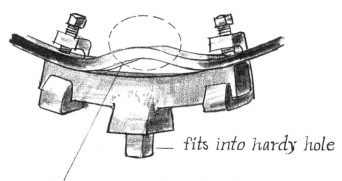

fits into hardy hole

the kinked part is heated red hot

first wheel—one on the wood rim and another on the iron tire—two double marks on the next wheel, and so on, he did a double job of marking that told him to which wheel each tire belonged, and also where each wheel belonged on the wagon. Wheels were sometimes removed beginning with the left front, moving on to the left rear, and on around to the front again, for it was thought bad luck for the smith to step over the wagon tongue.

In cases where the spokes and mortise joints were so badly worn that they could no longer be mended with simple remedies, the entire wheel was dismantled, after first being marked with numbers on all the pieces, for handmade wheels were not assembled from interchangeable parts. Each piece was examined, and corrective measures were taken: new spokes where needed, new felloes fitted, perhaps the tapered ends of spokes wrapped with canvas strips and glue to restore their proper diameter. Time-consuming as this was, it was still cheaper than a new wheel that might take a month to get from the factory and then not be exactly the right diameter after all.

The services of the smith were not always necessary. A good hard kick or some other expression of brute strength often did the trick, as in the following account.

One evening a two wheel cart drawn by a spirited bay horse came down Woodward Avenue. At Michigan, a coupé drove across the street directly in front of the rig, causing the driver to suddenly sheer off. As he did so, the tire of his wheel caught on a paving block and the wheel was dished back. The horse was caught by a passerby and held onto as the owner ruefully looked at his wheel, which was a new one. Policeman Wag . . . came up, and calling on one or two onlookers to assist him, succeeded in pulling the rim into place, and setting the wheel up as it had been before. "That makes five wheels I've straightened on this same corner," said the policeman. The owner thanked him, got in and drove off.*

measuring with a tracing wheel

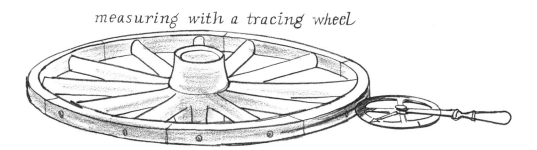

Before making a new iron tire, the blacksmith had first to measure the circumference of the rim with a tracing wheel, a light iron wheel about eight inches in diameter, fitted with a wooden handle, an adjustable pointer, and having a mark filed in the edge. After the blacksmith had made a chisel mark on the rim of the wagon wheel, the tracing wheel was set on the rim of the wagon wheel so that both marks lined

* From M. T. Richardson, *Practical Carriage Building.*

up exactly. The blacksmith rolled the tracing wheel slowly around the circumference of the wheel, letting it ride on the rim, and counting the number of revolutions it made. When the tracing wheel again came round to the chisel mark, the smith stopped and set the pointer to match the mark. Now the precise measurement was easy: It was equal in length to the number of revolutions plus the extra distance between the mark on the tracing wheel and its pointer. A piece of iron for the new tire could then be measured off by repeating this operation, rolling the tracing wheel along as before. After allowing a bit extra for the weld, the smith cut off the iron. Experience alone told him how much iron the weld would take. Trial and error had provided a rough formula: an amount of iron about equal to three times the thickness of the tire. For a tire made of quarter-inch stock, he added an extra three-fourths of an inch to its length.

The flat strip of iron was formed into a ring by cranking it through a tire-bending press, the pressure from the center gears forcing the metal into a curve. Both ends were then upset and scarfed, and the weld made. If all went well, the blacksmith had a perfectly round tire that would fit just right. When the job was done, the smith tested his work by hammering the tire at several points. The sound of iron on iron brought to his ears either the clear, bell-like ring of a wheel well ironed, or the hollow thud of failure.

A few smithies were equipped with a homemade version of the wheelright's frame—a husky wood table where the wheel was laid flat on its side, with the hub hanging down in the center. Most wheel repairs, even to shrinking on the tire, were better done with the wheel flat on its side. The smiths in many shops, though, did the tire shrinking outdoors, blocking the wheel up on chunks of wood. The finished tire was laid on top of a pile of old lumber and sticks, and a bonfire was started. As the tire became cherry red, the smith and his helper seized it with tongs and lifted it aside and onto the wheel, where it was hammered down flush. Instantly, spirals of white smoke curled out of the cracks, whereupon the wheel was pitched into a big tub of cold water.

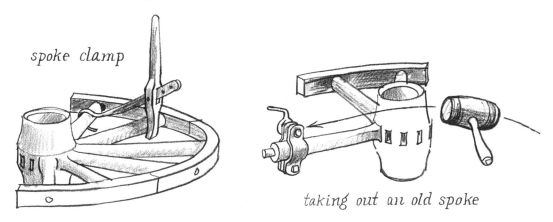

spoke clamp

taking out an old spoke

Indoors or out, the smith was perforce an innovator who exploited his ingenuity to get the job done faster, better, and thus more cheaply. For example, a particularly awkward task was that of putting in new felloes. The spokes, being rigid and well seated in the hub, were hard to force into the holes in the felloe. So the smith invented his own clamps, hooks, and levers to spring the spoke enough to let the felloe down into place.

Just as some of his welding joints were borrowed from the cabinet-maker and the carriage builder, so the blacksmith copied tools, adapted them, or created new ones, turning an idea into a laborsaving gadget with very little work at the anvil.

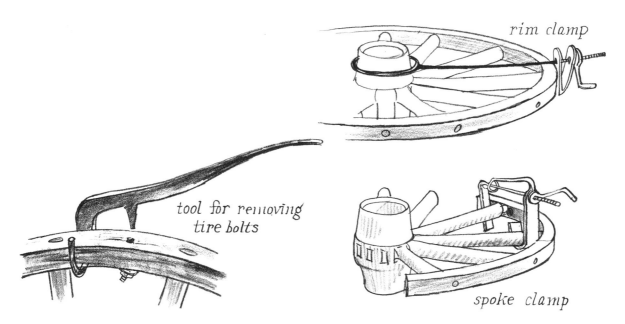

rim clamp

tool for removing tire bolts

spoke clamp

91

		Aug		
11	Mc Bentley Adsit		Chain Pd	50
			Horse	1 60
			New Axle	3 00
				6 1 0
12	Steven Bruver Mc E Adsit Doune Chas,		Chain &	
			hand nut	5 5
			S Points	60
			S Horse	90
			2 Tire	1 00
			New "	200
			Cha "	43 5
13	Jonson Douny Fresha Benjaman Slisone Mc Turner Hyde		2 Shoes	20
			Bolt & Hand nut	35
			Sharp	36
			S Horse	125
			Set Tire	200
			Hand nut	15
			2 Shoes	26
			S Horse	125
				5 85

The Blacksmith in His World

9

The villages of New England were effectively isolated from the outside world by topographic features and a general lack of transportation. The railroad had established a web of commercial contact among the larger cities, but the horse and wagon was a connecting link with a limited range, not much more extensive than from farm to village to railroad junction. By necessity, the inhabitants of each village provided for virtually all their own needs, having had the foresight to include in their number a shoemaker, a miller, carpenters, mill operators, a store-keeper or two, and a blacksmith. This tiny nucleus of artisans varied from town to town, depending on the lay of the land, proximity to water power, and other natural resources. Mill towns sprang up along the brooks; another town developed a specialty for marble or slate; others were entirely agricultural, the village forming the hub of quite an extensive farming area.

The blacksmith was early recognized as one tradesman who was almost indispensable to the survival of the community. In fact, of all the artisans, the smith possibly answered the greatest number of the villagers' needs. Every one of his neighbors needed something made of iron, whether for the farm, the sawmill, the woods, or the granite quarry. His trade brethren on the coast worked at making anchors and ships' hardware, or catered to such special industries as whaling, gunsmithing, and eventually the nut-and-bolt factories. Some even worked up to becoming foremen who tended power-driven forging machines in the factories. Coopers, hoe and edge-tool makers, locksmiths, cutlers, ornamental ironworkers, and instrument makers—all shared with the village blacksmith the basic knowledge of wrought iron and its manipulation.

The first party of settlers that came to Jamestown, Virginia, in 1607 included a blacksmith by the name of James Reed. By the end of the very next year another smith was needed, and in 1611, to meet the growing demand for ironworkers, four more smiths were sent over by the London-based Virginia Company. New England towns also acknowledged the importance of this craftsman, as shown in the Derby, Connecticut, town records for 1711:

> Voted, that the Town grant John Smith of Milford, blacksmith, four acres of land for a home lot, to build upon, anywhere within one mile of the meetinghouse where he shall choose, in land not laid out, upon condition that he build a mansion house [a dwelling] and smith's shop, and set up the trade of blacksmith, and follow it for the benefit of the inhabitants for the space of seven years.

The townspeople were clearly not meant to have to travel far to the blacksmith shop. But locating the forge practically next door to the church was no guarantee that the blacksmith would enjoy the same position in the community as the pastor, even if the villagers spent more time in his shop than they did in the meetinghouse. Piety was a trait no more frequently found among blacksmiths than among millhands, farmers, or any other group for that matter. Some, to be sure, sat on the pastoral supply committee when a new minister was being sought, but by the same token others probably never once set foot in the church to attend midweek prayer meeting. If he did become a pillar of society, as selectman, deacon, town clerk, fence viewer, grand juror, or overseer of the poor, the blacksmith achieved that status by the same means as any other townsman.

He charged his customers according to the pounds of iron used and for the time spent working it up; his base fee was generally the same for everyone. His cash earnings might reach the neighborhood of two thousand dollars and, counting payments in kind, he did rather well, as the following listing indicates.

Selected credit entries: items received in lieu of cash for blacksmithing services. From an unknown blacksmith's account book, Forbes Library, Northampton, Massachusetts.

1841	Mar	24	by cloth	5.87
		29	by pans	3.01
	Apr	1	by 1 pr boots	3.25
	May	24	by 7 lbs cast steel	1.40
	Aug	16	by ½ cord Wood	1.00
	Sep	8	by 20 bush cole	3.85

		14	by apples	.45
		18	by straw chips & wood	.20
	Oct	9	by 2¼ lb. c. steel	.45
		17	by 3 bush¹ potatoes	1.00
	Nov	16	by 180 lb. of old iron	2.60
	Dec	8	by 28 lbs mutton at 3½	.98
1842	Apr	26	by 1 pig	1.50
	May	3	by 15 lb. veal	.52
			by 1¼ cord Wood	2.50
		13	begun to pasture cow	
	Jul	10	by 75 lb rods	4.75
			by due bill given up	3.85
	Aug	25	by saw	.50
	Nov	9	by 24½ lbs old iron	.49
	Dec	14	by killing hog	.50
		31	by Pasturing cow 19 weeks	7.13

Good or bad, rich or poor, they were all his customers. They congregated at the smithy at all hours of the day and for various reasons. While the mare was being shod, there was time for talk, for argument, political debate, gossip, and ridicule. A lot of horse trading was done by the glow of the forge. Town meeting issues were aired and discussed before, and complained of after, the meeting. For young boys, the blacksmith shop held an attraction of quite a different sort. When not in school, or forced to stay home to fill the woodbox, they edged into the fringe of the group of bystanders just to listen, learn, and gape. To them, the smithy was a place of mystery and excitement, full of good sounds and smells.

The blacksmith, so far as any records show, never signed his work or even marked it with a distinguishing stamp. He took his work seriously enough, yet apparently saw it in quite a different light than did the silversmiths and instrument makers of the day who nearly always stamped their work with an identifying mark. It would have been pointless, if not ludicrous, to affix his mark to a pair of horseshoes, yet had the smith foreseen the inflated prices some of his hardware would one day bring as antiques, he might have been tempted to try it.

Longfellow pictures his blacksmith as a man of giant proportions, brawny enough to have picked a horse off the ground singlehanded or to have bent a piece of cold iron into a hoop with his bare hands. Though even the best of them might have fallen short of Longfellow's portrayal, many a smith actually was of powerful build. The majority of them were surely just ordinary human beings—tall and wiry or short and stocky; erect or stooped, young or old. And it was not uncommon to find at least the older smiths wearing spectacles, as a result of having worked for so many years in the dingy recesses of a shop with no artificial lighting. The scanty literature on blacksmiths and their ways mentions two men that Longfellow would probably have passed by completely, for one had a wooden leg and the other but one arm.

The word handmade when applied to a piece of work done on the anvil carried no implicit guarantee of quality. Not every hinge was perfect, not every wagon wheel stayed mended, and not every shoe held fast till worn out—which is to say that there were good smiths and bad ones. In fact, the acquisition of a new blacksmith was something of a gamble for a town. If the villagers chose well they would have at their service a true craftsman. If not, they might soon face the awkward necessity of sending him on his way and looking elsewhere.

Though most blacksmiths were not in the habit of keeping diaries or journals, a handful of them were in fact gifted in that direction. A few smiths spent considerable time in study and writing outside their own trade, while continuing to earn their living at the forge. Of these records, the letters and journals of Elihu Burritt are especially interesting. In the middle of Burritt's otherwise uneventful boyhood, he lost his father—who had been a soldier in the Revolutionary War—and was left on his own. At twenty-two, while apprenticed to the village blacksmith, one Samuel Booth, Burritt began to educate himself by studying Italian, Spanish, German, and Hebrew. In one of his letters to Longfellow he wrote: "I prefer to stand in the ranks of the workingman of New England and beckon them onward and upward to the full stature of intellectual men."

Elihu himself lived up to this philosophy. In 1843, he undertook the translation into English of a Spanish work, for which the publisher, Little, Brown and Company, Boston, paid him fifty cents a page. With the proceeds—two hundred dollars—Burritt bought books for his further studies. Meanwhile, he continued to "stand in the ranks of the workingman":

> *August 21, 1841*   Very warm, faint weather; feel sweaty and worn out; have been absent from my work only two days during the last five months. Congress has passed a great bankrupt bill which, a few days ago, they laid upon the table for the session. Studied Armenian. Have forged for eleven hours.
> *August 23*   Have forged 8 pruning hooks which I may sell next spring. Captain Holbrook delivered a most interesting lecture on temperance this evening.
> *September 22*   Wrote half the day. Hired a forge and began to prepare it for making garden utensils. I have given up the idea of removing from Worcester this fall. My money is all gone, therefore, if I should be sick I should be in an unpleasant predicament.
> *October 7*   . . . Got trusted for thirty pounds of cast steel to make my garden hoes of. Went to the library and read two and one half hours. Forged from one to five p.m.

Tuesday, May 23, 1843   In the afternoon I forged five
hoes in three hours. Spent the evening in my rooms.*

Burritt was challenged by the issues of his day, and in the course of
studying them he acquired many distinguished and stimulating new
friends. Among them were Henry Wadsworth Longfellow; Amasa
Walker, Secretary of State in Massachusetts; James Clark, a Quaker
leather merchant of Somerset; Lord John Russell, British Prime Minister; and Harriet Beecher Stowe, with whom he engaged in earnest discussion of the issues in the Civil War.

There were other blacksmiths who had to their credit the experience
of many years at the forge, and whose unusual inventiveness gave them
an interest in new methods as well as better ways of teaching the old
ones. From this group of smiths came a list of handbooks aimed at the
general public and at ironworkers, but more especially at trade schools.
In one such manual, after describing his own favored method of "dressing" an axe, the author had this to say:

> The axe factories with all their skill in hardening com-
> pounds have to do a better job yet to compete with me and
> my simple method.
>
> . . . By gather gauge I mean that the wheels [wagon]
> should be from ¼ to ½ inch wider at the back than the
> front. Don't misunderstand me now: I don't mean that the
> hind wheels should be wider than the front wheels. I mean
> that a wheel should have a little *gather* in the front as they
> are inclined to spread and throw the bearing on the nut,
> while, if they have a little gather, they will run right, and
> have a tendency to throw the bearing on the collars of the
> axle.†

Some said it better than others, however, as the next extract will indicate:

> Two of us did nothing all day except shoe. We started at
> six in the morning and went on till six in the evening, some-
> times till seven. The master smith were an old man over
> eighty. In his later years he didn't come into the smithy till
> after breakfast. The first man in the smithy in the morning
> had to pick up a hammer and strike the anvil three times—
> just to let the old man know we were there.
>
> I was always on shoeing. . . . We took two old shoes,

* From Merle Curti, *The Learned Blacksmith: The Letters and Journals of Elihu
Burritt.*
† From J. G. Holmstrom, *Modern Blacksmithing and Horseshoeing.*

heated them and hammered them together, the strikers striking alternately, the smith holding the shoes on the anvil and using a small hammer himself. During the twelve-hour day the two of us aimed to do thirty-six shoes, that is nine horses. Two of us averaged four shoes an hour. . . . The Town horses were nearly always leg weary and so were harder to shoe. They'd lie down on you as you lifted their leg.

. . . I was so tired I had to get off my bike twice on the way home and sit . . . in the snow before I could continue.*

Yet even as blacksmiths were expounding the fine points of dressing an axe, and waxing literary over the amount of gather in the front wheels of a wagon, momentous events were taking place in other parts of America. In 1892, six years before A. W. Dollar published his book *A Handbook of Horseshoeing,* a man in Iowa by the name of John Froelich manufactured and sold a successful gasoline-powered tractor, which started its builder in a business that was later bought out by the John Deere Plow Company, today one of the largest manufacturers of farm machinery in the country. And in April of the following year— 1893—Henry Ford was road-testing his first gasoline-driven automobile.

Radical changes were taking place throughout the nation—changes that would affect the blacksmith, the shoemaker, the mill operator, the storekeeper, and even life itself in the quiet villages.

* From Garry Hogg, *Hammer and Tongs: Blacksmithery Down the Ages.*

1904 Ford

Building a Forge

10

There is no doubt that the end of the horse-and-buggy era brought with it the virtual disappearance of the village blacksmith. But it is now evident—a great many years later—that what vanished was not the blacksmith, but his *particular role* in society. Something new has happened: influenced by economics and the realization that unless it's homemade they may never have it, people have discovered they can indeed do a great many things for themselves.

Men and women who thought they didn't have thumbs, let alone green ones, have taken to gardening and are successfully putting by food for the winter. There are more carpenters around these days than you can shake a stick at—erstwhile electronics engineers, stockbrokers, secretaries, television specialists, housewives, and Harvard graduates. Young men and women are struggling to own land, and are then facing the problem of making a living on it, not always by commuting fifty miles to an office job, but by performing for themselves many of the services which a high standard of living once taught us to believe could only be bought with cash.

Along with the stonemason, the builder of post and beam houses, the one-family farmer, the potter, and the carpenter, the blacksmith appears to be returning. Scores of new ironworkers, most of them graduates of accredited courses offered in colleges and universities, are hanging out their shingles. Why? Certainly not because these new craftsmen are naive enough to believe this trade is any guarantee to wealth. It isn't. Although it may be a stereotyped phrase, there is evidence of a steady return to older values—inner human values.

Tradition, craftsmanship, pride in solid methods and principles—qualities once inconspicuous because they were routine requirements—must be exerting considerable influence, however intangible.

It is quite affecting to know that you alone are responsible for the staircase that hasn't a squeak in it; that you framed the roof over your head to carry the load of winter snow; that the door latch under your thumb came from the anvil in the back shed; that the eggs in the skillet stand up proud "on their hind legs" because you fed the hens yourself and didn't turn on a light bulb to make them work all night. Door latch or a brace of eggs—both are part of something that fortunately cannot be explained.

Why go to all the work of building a forge when one can be ordered from a catalogue—complete with an iron bowl and a firepot, tuyère, gear-driven blower (hand-operated or electric), and four legs for it to stand on? They even have fancy hoods. Why not just buy one, line the pan with fireclay, and plug in the blower cord? Another question comes quickly to mind: Why pick blacksmithing for a trade? There are other ways to make a living—with a lot less grime and probably shorter hours. This chapter and the one that follows it are for the ingenious mechanic who finds it a challenge to build things himself, to use what he can readily lay hands on, and who extracts a peculiar satisfaction from it all. He'll spend less money and derive a greater amount of pleasure from working a forge that is in every detail his own, just as the man who built his own sloop finds a sweetness in sailing her that the wealthy yachtsman may completely miss. In the country, you can generally find nearly all the materials from which to build a good, solid forge—planks, locust posts, bricks, stone, an old iron sink (for the pan) or enough iron to weld one together. Anyone clever enough and with the good sense to be a blacksmith probably has the necessary ingenuity and skill. And besides the satisfaction of having built it himself, he may also find an exhilaration in having become part of a tradition.

In many cases, it may be quite true: whatever comes out of a factory can be improvised or made, at home. The factory product followed in the wake of handwork—in shape, construction, and function an imitation of the homemade article. With a few basic tools a man can build his own forge, a double-chamber bellows with leather "lungs," and a serviceable chimney. An ingenious person could even devise and make his own tuyère, though it's questionable if it is worth the time.

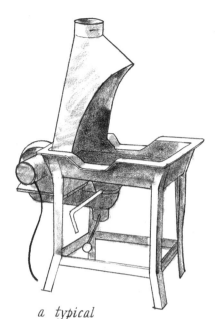

*a typical
pressed steel hearth
with electric blower*

PLANNING THE BUILDING AND SPACE

There was once a man who claimed he could build a river steamboat without so much as a "rough idee" scratched on an old board, but for most of us, some preliminary planning is almost indispensable. Every

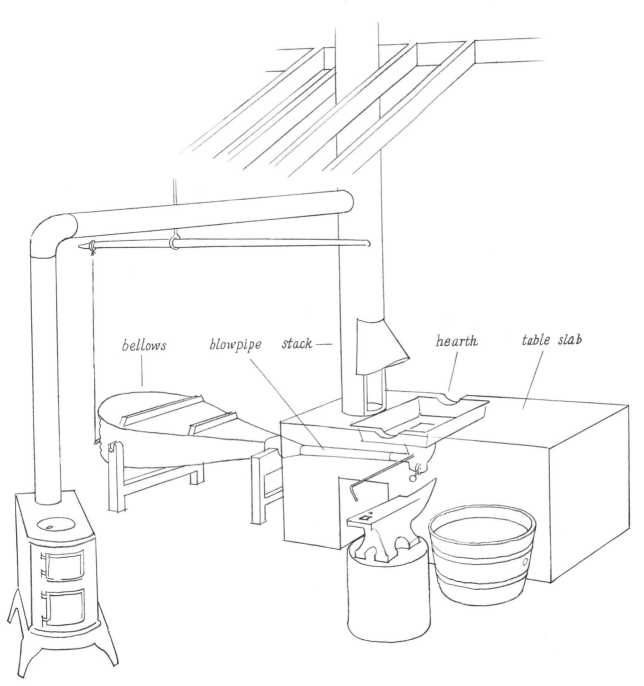

bellows   blowpipe stack —   hearth   table slab

construction job has its booby traps, most of which stay pretty well hidden until the work is far advanced. However, a lot of them can be smoked out on paper, with a little patience and pencil work.

A forge is not the easiest thing to move or to change radically, once it's been built, so it's well to get everything figured out ahead of time, preferably with the help of some scale drawings. A scale drawing is not difficult to make: an ordinary 12-inch ruler is the only tool required. A useful scale is 1½ inches to one foot. That will mean ⅛ inch equals an inch, and the sixteenths will represent half inches, which is quite fine enough for the job.

Aside from providing the blacksmith with the creature comforts, some building is essential to shelter the forge and everything that goes with it. At this planning stage the problem comes down to fitting together two sets of facts: the space the forge will take up and the amount of space in the building. To put it another way, how to fit what you need into the building you've got. If the forge is to be built in a brand new building, this problem doesn't exist. However, it's more likely that a barn, corncrib, shed, garage, sugar house, or back room is the only space available, and now the only question is: how to get everything into it?

The answer probably won't come from the first set of drawings. But, to spare the necessity of duplicating drawings over and over again, make a floor plan of the building on one sheet of paper—any roll paper is good because it can be any length—and a drawing of the forge on another, using tracing paper. The tracing can be laid over the floor plan and shifted around until as many of the requirements as possible seem to have been covered, and the tracing then taped down. The floor plan of the building should show (to scale) the location of rafters, windows, doors, stairs, and any supporting posts or other immovable obstructions.

Even so, this is a trial-and-error exercise, and it may be that some parts of the forge equipment will have to be relocated. Generally speaking, though, the forge is one continuous unit: bellows, blowpipe, stack, hearth, and table slab. Also, it is important for handy work at the forge to have the anvil and slack tub set in the right spots, so these should be included on the tracing paper overlay. It isn't absolutely essential to have the bellows behind the stack. In many shops it was set up to one side, but usually on the *same side* of the forge as the anvil. This is because the bellows pole lever must be within the smith's reach.

There are other appurtenances of a blacksmith shop that are indispensable, and probably the best way to plan space for them—or try to—is by making a list:

Walk space Space clear around the forge to accommodate long pieces of iron, plus space around the bellows for making repairs. A three-foot-wide walk space is ideal.
Storage Anvil tools, iron stock, wood and lumber, and "junk," something that every hand workman either collects or should.
Workbench Woodworking tools, vise, clamps, bench grinder, tools needed for the work you expect to do.
Fabricating space Plenty of floor space to work on large jobs such as wagons and farm implements.

104

Table slab   An essential for any kind of work, handy place
to flop out a piece of red-hot iron or to assemble small
jobs. Best if smooth and level.

Stove   Almost essential in cold climates: heat from the forge
roasts the face and hands, but warms little else. The stovepipe can go into the forge chimney, but have it high
enough so you don't bang your head on it.

In spite of all this, it may develop that the building isn't big
enough, and something will have to be sacrificed. The question is,
what? The working parts of the forge must stay, and by all means,
the so-called fabricating space. That leaves walk space, storage and
stove. Since I live where I do, and my feet get cold, I would keep
the stove. But, don't set it up too near the bellows; the leather will
dry out. Keep as much walk space as possible, which pretty much
means storing materials someplace else: overhead, in the peak of the
building; on the second floor, if it has one; in a lean-to outside; or in
some other building. An alternate solution would be a connected shed
which can be shut off in the winter, yet allow you to get materials
without plowing through the snow and cold. It's all according
to what you think you must have, and how much annoyance you're
willing to put up with.

Before starting construction, there is one key factor to be taken
into account: since the stack (or chimney) must go through the roof,
its position will obviously determine where the forge must be set.
Taking measurements from the scale drawing, cut a hole in the roof
between two rafters and to one side of the ridgepole. This is simpler
than centering the chimney, requires far less framing, and makes the
job of flashing the chimney easier as well. Hang a plumb line from
the center of this hole, with the plumb bob an inch or two off the
ground or floor. That is where the chimney goes; and with that point
established, everything else can be measured off and marked on the
floor or ground.

THE TUYÈRE: HEART OF THE FORGE

The term *forge* has more than one meaning. The early stone
furnace where iron ore was smelted was called a forge. A lot of the
old blacksmith shops went by the name of forge, too. Getting down
to the more particular, the word forge was quite often used to
mean just the fire in a blacksmith shop. As a matter of fact and
tradition, forge probably takes in everything needed to do ironwork:
the hearth (which includes the pan, firepot, and tuyère), the chimney,
bellows, blowpipe, and any embellishments such as tool racks and a
table slab for cooling hot iron. Not, of course, forgetting the anvil
and slack tub. But because many of these appurtenances have been

105

elaborated elsewhere, the more limited meaning of *forge* will be used here to include the hearth, chimney, bellows, and the construction to put it on.

A graphic description of the fundamentals of a forge comes from Kenneth Lynch, proprietor of the ironworking firm of Kenneth Lynch & Sons, of Wilton, Connecticut:

> Basically if you just had a hole in the ground and a tube running to that hole and a blower of some kind to induce air in the tube, you would have just as good a forge as anyone. However, when you wanted to clean the fire you would have to pull the whole business out on top to clean it. The poor blacksmith would have to squat down in order to use the fire.

Fundamentally, a forge is nothing more than a box to hold the fire, with a tuyère bolted on underneath, raised to a comfortable working height, and provided with an air blast to develop higher temperatures than the fire alone can generate. It is possible to do some limited ironwork in an open fireplace, just as maple sap can be crudely evaporated over a campfire without benefit of an iron arch and special fluepans. However, that is about the limit. A deep bed of coals may look hot enough to work iron, and indeed it will often produce a cherry red temperature. But it will never by itself reach the pale yellow or white color necessary for a compete range of forging, which must include welding heat.

A simple experiment will demonstrate the necessity of a forced air blast. Burn a good hot fire in a fireplace (using oak, ash, maple, or hickory) until there is a deep bed of coals. Lay a short length of two-inch iron pipe from the hearth into the center of the coals. Insert a vacuum cleaner tube into the pipe and start the motor. The air blast will be much too strong, but the rise in fire temperature will be impressive, observed as a color change in the coals from dull yellow, to lemon, and then to white.

It is a proven fact: the tuyère is a vast improvement over a simple air tube at the base of the fire. This strange-looking piece of cast iron with its rotating valve and lever is probably the most important part of the whole forge, and the one piece of equipment that should be bought ready-made. Better to have an efficient firepot hooked up to a crude forge than a beautiful pile of brickwork that won't work. Its design has evolved over a long, long time. It works. And it saves the blacksmith a lot of time and, nowadays, money. While the price of a tuyère today is several times what it was in the horse-and-buggy era, it is still one of the best investments a smith can make.

> The tuyère is not merely a novelty developed by some blacksmith, but it is a scientific mechanical device not only

permitting you to keep the ashes out of the air tube but also
it permits you to preheat the air by blowing it around the
inner body of the tuyère before blowing it up into the coal.
    . . . a tuyère with a hot air space in it will heat the iron
in one third less time and with a good deal less coal.
—Kenneth Lynch

The Buffalo Forge Company, in their eight hundred eleventh catalogue—the company dates back to the 1800s—describes the merits of
one of their models listed at $165:

Its eccentric blast valve offers a wide range of regulations as
follows:
    To produce a large deep fire, the blast is forced into the fire
pot through three tapering converging channels.

cross section of firepot with tuyère and ash gate

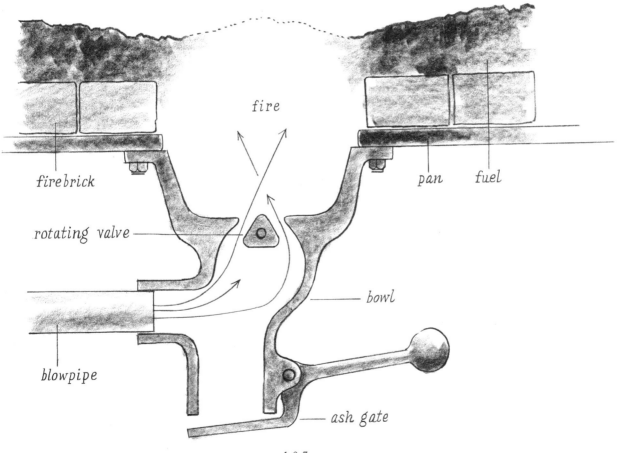

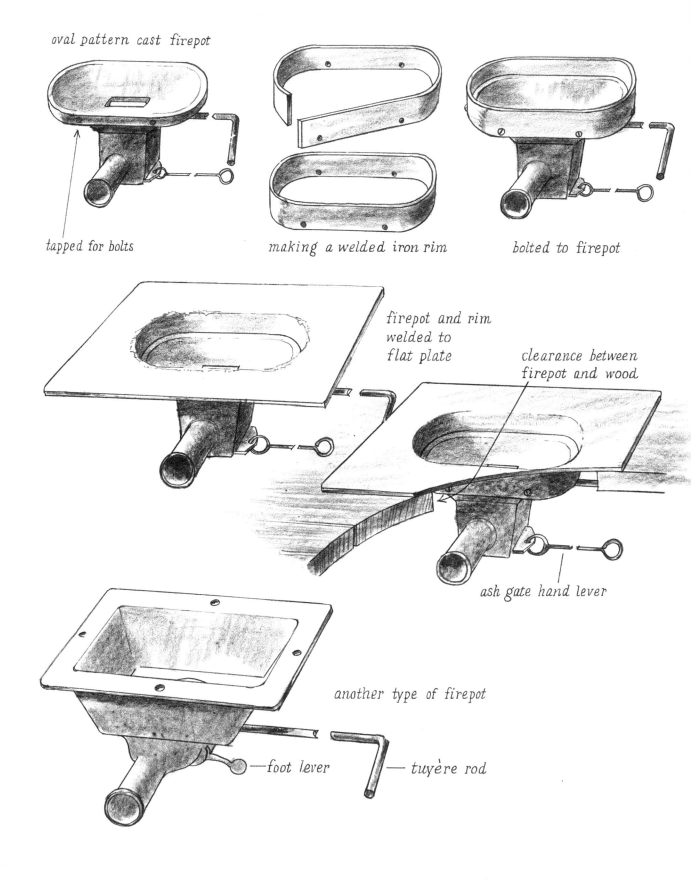

oval pattern cast firepot

tapped for bolts

making a welded iron rim

bolted to firepot

firepot and rim
welded to
flat plate

clearance between
firepot and wood

ash gate hand lever

another type of firepot

foot lever — tuyère rod

A quarter turn of the rod will bring the valve to a position for a small fire at either side of the firepot. Because of the rising and falling action of the valve (the eccentric), it is easy to break up clinkers and clean the fire pot. Cleaning out from the top is unnecessary.

[This] firepot has a clinker breaking valve as well as a hinged and balanced ash gate which opens and closes by a touch of the foot.

A good firepot with a tuyère and an ash gate may cost about the equivalent of twenty to thirty paid working hours at the anvil. Constructing a forge entails considerable work—regardless of how rudimentary in design. Since the whole idea is a hot fire, and a firepot with tuyère the most efficient way to get it, the initial purchase price is relatively low, and a sound investment. The amount of money spent will seem small compared to the anguish and frustration of a home-made gadget, especially if it doesn't work very well. And replacing it later on with a store-bought unit would mean tearing the whole forge apart.

DETERMINING THE SIZE OF THE HEARTH

Since the hearth is the soul of the forge, and its size must be determined before the pan and the supporting structure can be built, the place to begin measuring and calculating is around the sides of the firepot with its built-in tuyère. The pan will have to be lined with fire-resistant material, the ideal being firebrick, which is designed to withstand exceedingly high temperatures. Common red brick will work, the older the better, as a higher proportion of sand was used in brick made, for example, in the 1800s. Even so, common brick does deteriorate in fire, and will have to be replaced at intervals. Firebrick costs more and is considerably larger than common old brick, but this is a drawback only if the two kinds are worked together. A less expensive solution is to line the floor of the pan with firebrick—where the heat is greatest—laying up the sides with old red brick. Perhaps it really comes down to the question of thrift, as expressed by one builder:

> I built the whole thing [forge] out of a couple of chimneys I picked up just to cart them away, and a pair of good iron cranes thrown in. Fire brick would be better, but I didn't have any, or money to buy it. There's enough left in that pile to make repairs for some time to come.
> —Silas Hyde, Sandisfield, Massachusetts

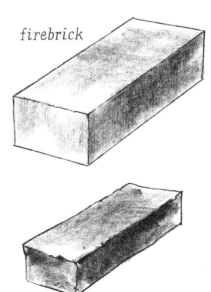

firebrick

old common red brick

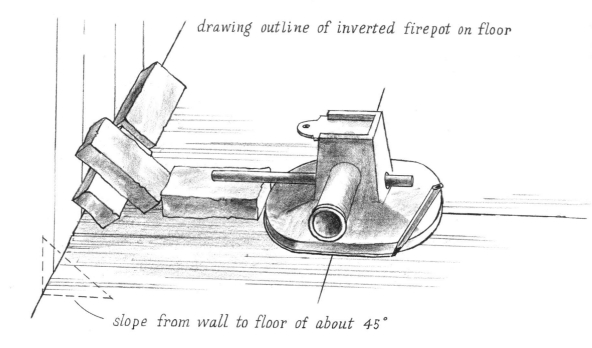

drawing outline of inverted firepot on floor

slope from wall to floor of about 45°

With the actual firepot in your possession—and it's best not to try making calculations until it is—lay the firepot bottom side up on the floor next to a wall and draw a chalk or pencil outline around it. Mark off center lines in both directions. Have 85 or 90 bricks at hand, of the size and kind that will go into the actual construction. Start fitting bricks around the edges of the chalk outline on the floor, adding bricks until the hearth is the size wanted. Scraps of heavy carton cardboard can be stuck between bricks to represent the mortar. The time thus spent will provide realistic dimensions consistent with standard unit measurements—whole bricks and half bricks—and avoid having to cut a lot of odd-length pieces. One that I laid out, using a 15-inch oval firepot and secondhand red brick, measured 35 inches wide and 47 inches from front to back. These measurements represent the inside dimensions of the pan.

Another trial can easily be made to decide on the total depth of the hearth (and hence the fire), as measured from the tuyère slot to the top edge of the hearth. Set up the firepot on some temporary base and lay in firebrick around it without any mortar. Lay up the sides of the hearth the same way. Build a fire and try it out. From this dry-run layout the final dimensions can be taken off. This system is much better than relying exclusively on a scale drawing, because it is three-dimensional and gives a better feel of the true size.

When laying out the brick in this "floor trial," give some thought to which brick-laying pattern is best. Having the bricks "bonded," or tied together, is just as important here as it would be in a wall. Stagger the joints and work out a pattern with as few half bricks as possible.

As to the final size of the hearth and pan, there are a few questions the answers to which will provide useful information. What sort of work will the forge do? Theoretically, as some say, there is little sense in building a great deep pan if the only work is going to be small hardware. I disagree. It's quite true that no one can be prepared for every eventuality, let's say by building a forge that will accommodate butterfly hinges as well as cannon. On the other hand, it is a lot easier to build a small fire in a large pan than it is to attempt the opposite, and suppose somebody comes along to have a wagon axle straightened, and the hearth is no bigger than a horseshoe?

What heft of iron will be used? Not every small wrought iron article is necessarily made of thin stock, and it seems almost unnecessary to point out that the thicker the iron the deeper the fire required to heat it.

laying out a trial hearth on the floor

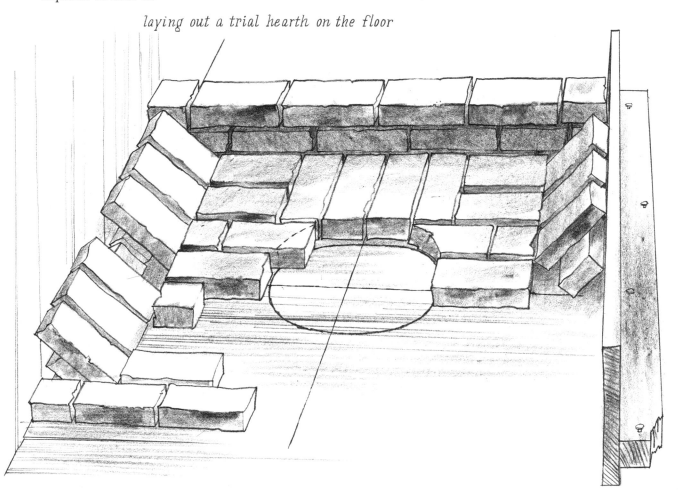

What is the capacity of the bellows? Somewhere, it seems, there must be figures for nearly everything under the sun. But not this. An electrically driven blower is one thing; a double-chamber leather lung bellows is something else, but it will run a fair-sized fire, and a small one, too. This could be tested to yield reasonably accurate data by operating a blower or a bellows in a fireplace fire *before* the final apparatus is built.

On the whole, bigger is probably better, along with a size of hearth to match the output of the bellows.

Getting back to the mock-up on the floor, continue laying out bricks until the hearth looks big enough for your needs. Two courses of brick above the level of the inside will make a pan about four and a half inches deep. This, with the area over the firepot sunk the thickness of another brick, makes possible a fire depth of something like eight inches.

From this finished model, final measurements can be taken off and used to build the wooden skeleton to hold up this brickwork.

BUILDING THE FORGE STRUCTURE

With the dimensions of the hearth established, the structure to contain all the parts of the forge can be built, of course, consulting the scale drawings and other information. It can be simple and strictly utilitarian, or designed with all the comforts of home: a table slab to one side of the hearth, a tool rack across the end, shelves and compartments underneath. Nowadays, a hanging fluorescent shop light would be handy. It is all according to what is wanted, the time and money available, and the kind and volume of work anticipated.

No doubt disagreement will arise about many of the dimensions and proportions shown in the illustrations. The fact is, there is no single "correct" set of standard dimensions. The only guide is what works, and forges of all sizes, shapes, and descriptions have proven workable—from the hole-in-the-ground variety to the full-blown brick structure shown on page 100.

The main thing is to make the trials, and especially the errors, in advance. Work out sizes and building procedures ahead of time. Try out construction plans by making rough sketches if necessary. Then, once all the details are set, stick to them.

Must a forge be heavy? I think so. I like a good substantial forge resting on its base with solid, immovable weight. Some of the large factory-made pressed steel forges with tubular legs, electric blower, hood, and water tank, weigh about 475 pounds. The smaller, portable ones weigh as little as 40 pounds. The hearth and supporting base described here is built of hardwood plank, well-fastened to make a firm, heavy structure that will not fall over every time a big iron bar accidentally knocks it. This is the kind of forge that will generally result from *some variations in construction details*

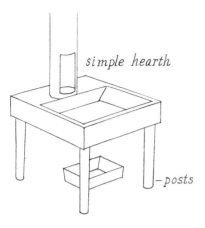

simple hearth

—posts

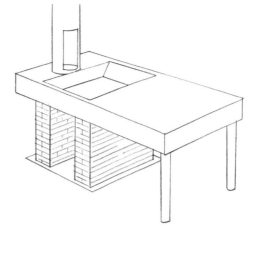

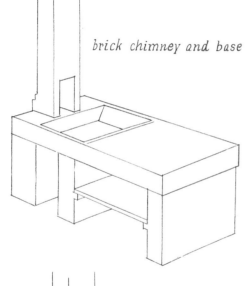

brick chimney and base

brick on sand

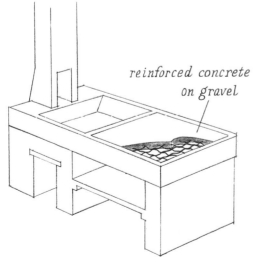

reinforced concrete on gravel

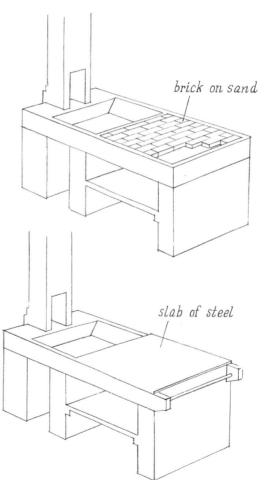

slab of steel

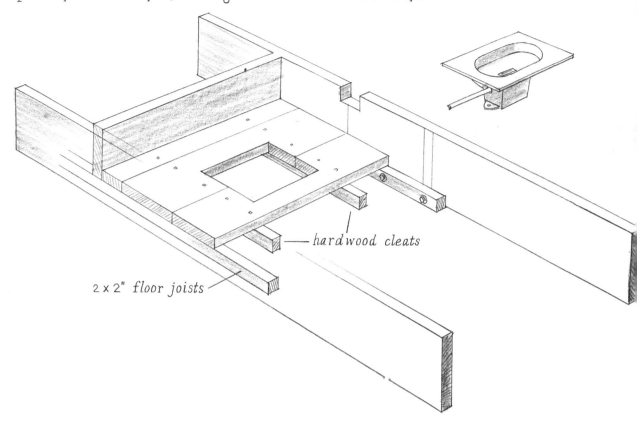

partially constructed pan, showing center cut out for the firepot

2 x 2" *floor joists*

hardwood cleats

having built it out out of whatever materials can be found around the place—planks, bricks, and posts.

The height of the forge is important. Even if the iron you'll be working with is not in itself inordinately heavy, standing all day in an awkward back-bent position is exhausting. As with determining the height of an anvil, it is worthwhile to do a little experimenting to find out what is the most comfortable. Pick up a pair of tongs and try out the height of the kitchen sink, a table, counter top, or workshop bench—any surfaces with which you are familiar—and jot down the measurements.

I would never build a hearth without some easy way of sliding long pieces of iron as deep into the fire as wanted. The old brick forges were built with a pair of slots—one in the back wall of the hearth, another in front—lined up on the center of the firepot. These were nothing more than gaps in the brickwork which could be closed by dropping in loose brick. In a hearth framed out of wood, front and back notches can be cut out to a depth of about four inches, and the lining brick left loose at these two places.

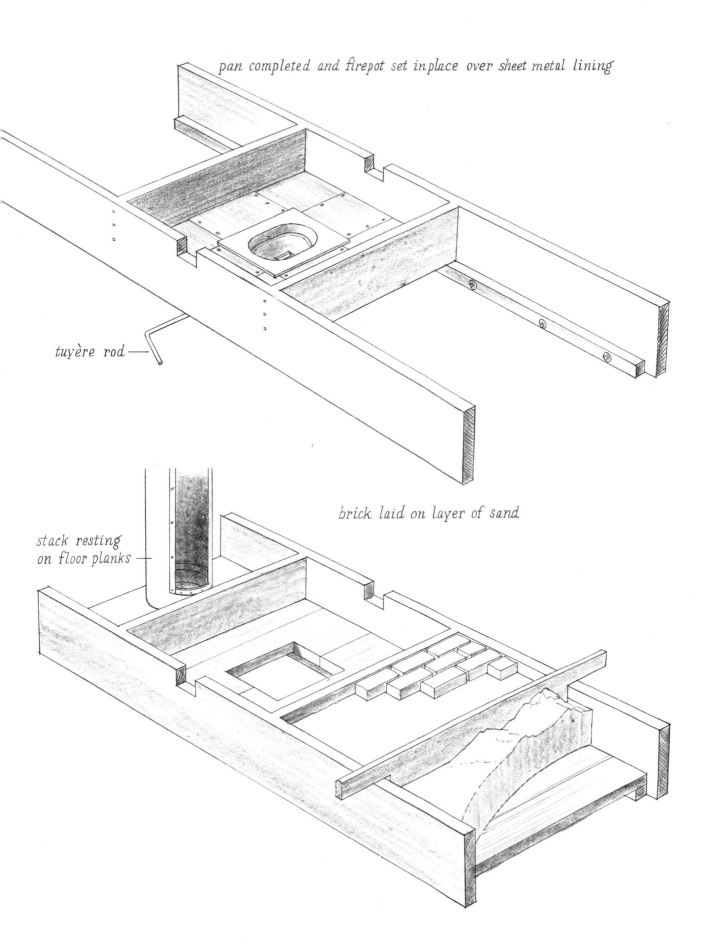

pan completed and firepot set in place over sheet metal lining

tuyère rod

brick laid on layer of sand

stack resting
on floor planks

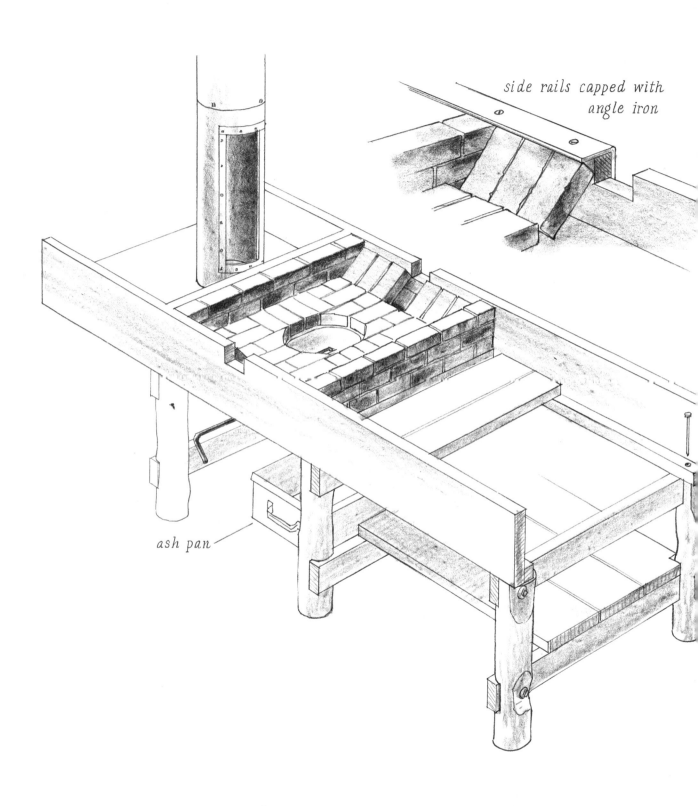

side rails capped with
angle iron

ash pan

A good stout pan—and the one described here—can be built of two-inch hardwood plank for the floor and sides, and supported on four locust posts about five or six inches in diameter, well-braced and fastened with bolts. A pan welded up out of flat and straight pieces of iron makes a good hearth. A flat slab of steel or an arrangement of closely spaced angle iron will also work—anything strong enough to hold the combined weight of the firepot, tuyère, firebrick, and fuel. An old iron sink would probably work, too, although by the time it was lined with brick, it would be quite a small hearth.

When the final dimensions are figured out, the position of the posts can be staked out or marked on the floor, making sure the corners are square.

In a building that is already floored-in, the forge can be set on the floor, but it would be well to replace the floor boards with plank—at least those under the forge—and see that the joists are heavy enough to carry the weight.

Many older farm buildings stand on stone foundations or corner posts, leaving the floor of dirt. In such a situation, in climates where extended periods of freezing or sub-zero temperatures expand and heave the ground, the posts supporting the forge should be set below frost line. In the Northeast, for example, this means at least four and a half feet below ground level. The post holes should be dug the full diameter of a standard shovel, or about 12 inches, so that a tamping stick such as a 2 x 4 will fit into the hole beside the post. After dropping the post

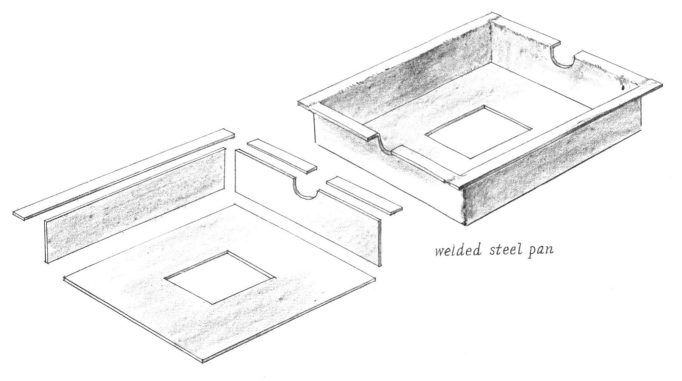

welded steel pan

117

cutting brick :

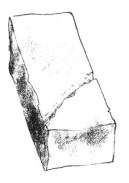

score both sides

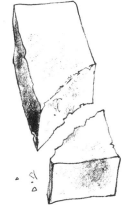

then —
a couple of
good whacks

into the hole, fill in three or four inches of dirt, and compact it well with the tamping stick. Add only a small amount of dirt at a time, using the tamper liberally. From time to time, check the plumb both ways with a level. When you think it's done—take a couple of last turns around the post with the tamper. The posts should now be good and tight.

Naturally, all notches and rabbets for the plank braces are cut before the posts are set. Getting these cuts properly lined up and level may require throwing in or scraping out a little dirt. With the posts set and the brace planks bolted in place, the hearth pan can be built and lined with brick.

LINING THE HEARTH

With the pan built and the firepot bolted into place under the hole cut for this purpose, the next step is to line the hearth, using the mock-up on the floor as a guide for laying in the brickwork.

Fireclay is probably better than regular mortar, although it's surprising how well makeshifts will work. Fireclay is a refractory compound used to line stoves, as protection against scaling and burning. Sold as an oatmeal-colored dry powder, it is prepared simply by mixing with water. For setting firebrick, the consistency should be the same as cement mortar, and the joints between bricks made about ¼-inch to ⅜-inch. When fireclay is used alone—without brick—to line a commercial pressed steel forge, use only enough water to make a stiff putty, and apply it as an even coating one half to one inch thick. A fire should be built the minute the work is done, as heat is necessary to cure the clay and set it up hard. It's not necessary to hook up the blower or bellows for this. Run the fire two or three hours until all the joints are cured.

Practically speaking, new firebrick could be laid-in without any mortar or fire clay: they are uniform in size and fit together very tightly. Still, the fireclay serves a purpose: it fills all the cracks between bricks, making a tight, solid, fireproof floor.

Although this brick lining probably provides sufficient insulation between the fire and the wooden box, a lining of light gauge sheet metal will add some further protection. The metal need not be all in one piece, so long as the joints are overlapped.

It's a good idea to bed the brick lining of the floor of the pan in fireclay: that is, butter the bottom of the brick to get a firm seat against the sheet metal lining. Other than this, lay in the brick, using fireclay as you would mortar. Don't forget to leave loose brick front and back for those long bars! When it comes to lining the front and back walls of the hearth, start with the loose brick, and to make sure they'll slip in and out easily, put a scrap of carton on either side before mortaring in the bricks next to them.

In most of the old brick forges, the ashes dropped into the ash pit under the hearth and were cleaned out from time to time. This same

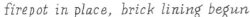

firepot in place, brick lining begun

fireclay mortar

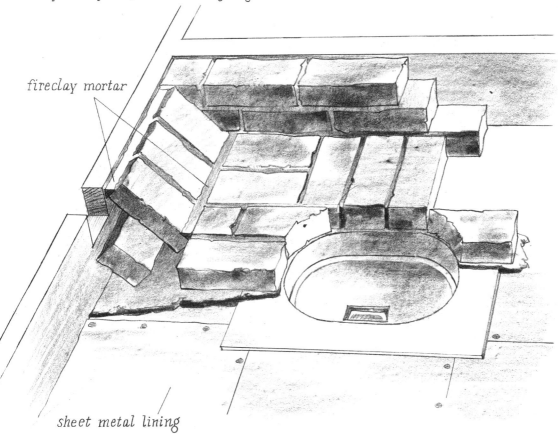

sheet metal lining

scheme still works, but it is not recommended where the floor is of wood. A five-gallon paint bucket makes a fair ash pan, or one can be put together from sheet metal and fitted with a carrying handle. Either one saves the trouble of shoveling ashes.

STACK AND CHIMNEY

A stack made of sheet metal works just as well as a brick or stone chimney, even if it may not look as pretty. So-called stovepipe is available from plumbing and heating shops in standard lengths and in various diameters. The sections should be set up with the crimped ends up, the first section fitting inside the one on top of it. Fasten each joint with at least three sheet metal screws. These do tend to rust and seize up tight. In one back-country shop, the blacksmith—because of the bitter cold—was in the habit of closing up shop in January and February and

1 1 9

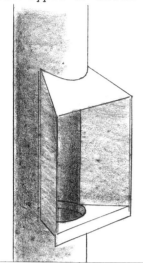

taking down the whole stack. He would periodically climb up a ladder and remove—then immediatley replace—all the sheet metal screws!

Whether sheet metal or brick, a chimney can be balky about taking the first gulp of smoke when the fire is started, especially on a cold winter morning. There may even be a down draft. A few newspapers wadded up and burned in the flue hole will quickly remedy this. If the forge fire is lighted at the same time, everything should begin working. Although many of the old forges were equipped with hoods, presumably to collect and funnel the smoke into the chimney, the draft alone ought to take care of the problem. Attaching a hood could be delayed and added later on after you see how well the stack draws.

In order to guarantee that the smoke will be drawn into the flue (and not blown into your face), the stack should be set right against one side of the hearth—all this having been worked out on paper.

A flue hole (the opening into the stack) must be cut out of the bottom end of the first section: a rectangle *on one side only,* which will face the hearth. Cutting the hole will be easier if the lock-seam is slid apart and the section of stovepipe partially flattened out on a bench (not hammered out).

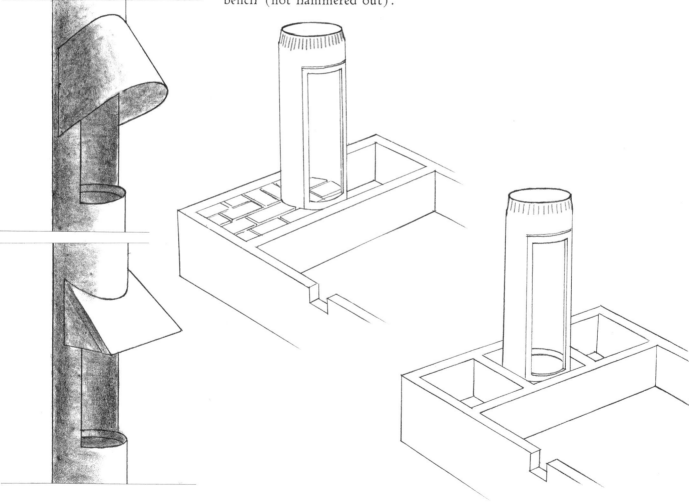

Once a round stovepipe is cut, it loses its tubular rigidity. The edges of the flue hole will therefore have to be stiffened. Bend a ring of flat bar iron (about ⅛ x ¾) that will fit snugly inside the base of the stovepipe, and rivet it into place. The three edges of the flue hole could be stiffened by turning them into flanges, but a neater way is to rivet flat bar iron around all three sides. This seems to disturb the natural round of the pipe a good deal less. The piece across the top has to be bent to the same arc as the pipe itself.

After setting up this base section, the others can be set up and the top end slid through the roof. Put off tapping in the sheet metal screws until the last; this will save time if it has to be taken down for any reason.

In the interest of having a good draft, the top of the stack should extend well above the ridge line of the building.

Where the stack goes through the roof, a flat piece of sheet metal fastened to one section of stovepipe makes a good thimble to protect the roof boards from the hot metal.

Make the flat sheet large enough to reach up under the course of shingles at the top, and to extend on both sides well back under the shingles. The lower edge lies on top of the shingles. Naturally, to fit a sloping roof, this gadget has to have an *oval* hole cut for the stack, a geometric puzzle best solved by making a cardboard pattern. The tabs around the center hole are bent up, fastened to the section of stack with sheet metal screws, and then the whole seam completely soldered.

On a brick chimney, flashing will have to be put on around the stack and worked into the layers of shingles. Sheet lead is the best material to use. Unlike aluminum, tin, or copper, it stretches without breaking and can be molded around masonry to get a very tight fit, even on corners where comparable results with these other, rigid materials would require soldering. Lead resists rust, corrosion, and fatigue cracks: for all practical purposes, it will last forever.

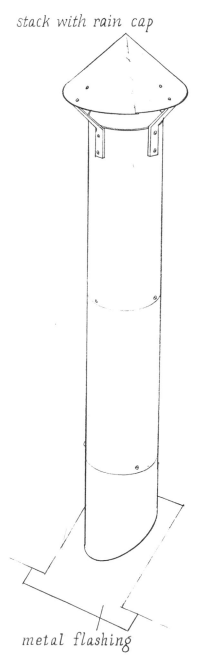

stack with rain cap

metal flashing

*flue opening
reinforced with
strap iron*

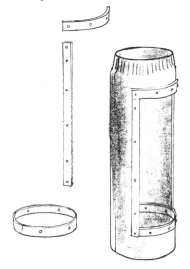

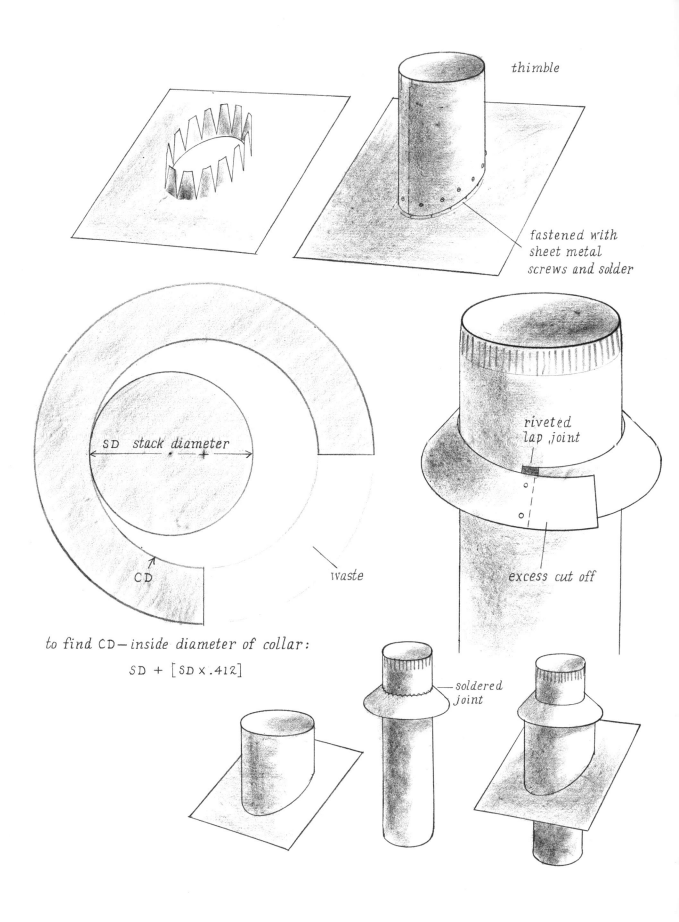

thimble

fastened with
sheet metal
screws and solder

riveted
lap joint

excess cut off

SD stack diameter

CD

waste

to find CD—inside diameter of collar:

SD + [SD × .412]

soldered
joint

It is a fine thing to work at a big forge, with the well-laid brick, the arched top over the ash pit, and the recessed compartment where a box of flux fits nicely. But why build something that massive when a simpler one works just as well, and costs less? Such a forge might require 3,500 brick, which, if bought new at twelve cents apiece, means an initial outlay of $420. Furthermore, the number of man-hours to build it will far exceed those spent on a less ambitious version.

There are a number of answers. For one thing, brick makes a structure of incomparable solidity that needs almost no maintenance. For another, it has a particularly shipshape appearance: it is attractive to look at. Aside from all this, working at an old-fashioned forge carries with it a feeling of being part of tradition, not unlike the satisfaction of using tools handed down from a great-grandfather. In the end, though, the best reason for building with brick may be strictly practical: You have a great heap of old brick stacked in the yard. Or you know where to get some for nothing—all the building material necessary and an unlimited supply of repair parts.

Old chimneys and foundation walls can still be found, either in burned-out cellar holes or standing in the wreckage of nearly collapsed houses. More and more often these days, perfectly sound brick buildings are being torn down to make way for progress, and a lot of this brick ends up in salvage yards or as landfill. Getting to the site ahead of the demolition squad, coupled with a knack for dickering, could result in a free supply of building material.

Secondhand brick of course has to be cleaned of old mortar, a job expeditiously done with a hatchet, and one that goes faster on the old, softer mortar which has less cement and more lime. As the brick are cleaned and sorted, save all the whole bricks, half bricks, and three-quarter lengths. These last are useful where odd lengths have to be cut. In batches of brick from burned-out buildings, there are usually a lot of flaky, crumbled brick that are useless for construction, but they can be used to help fill the excavation for the foundation.

All the foregoing admonitions and warnings about planning, scale drawings, and trial mock-ups apply here with even more emphasis. A grandiose brick forge could easily turn out to be a monument—and an indestructible one at that—to unchecked impulsiveness. In addition to laying everything out on paper, make dry-run trials as needed to determine dimensions, naturally using the unit size of the brick you have on hand. The older brick—even from the same kiln batch—varies quite a lot in size. In deciding on the total length of the forge, it is safest to lay out on the floor a test course of brick, allowing for mortar and then simply measure the whole thing. This is more sensible than starting with an arbitrary size, only to discover that you have to cut a quarter-length brick for every course!

Simple wooden forms can save a lot of consternation, too. Let's assume that the opening into the ash pit is to have a curved arch

floor plan of brick forge

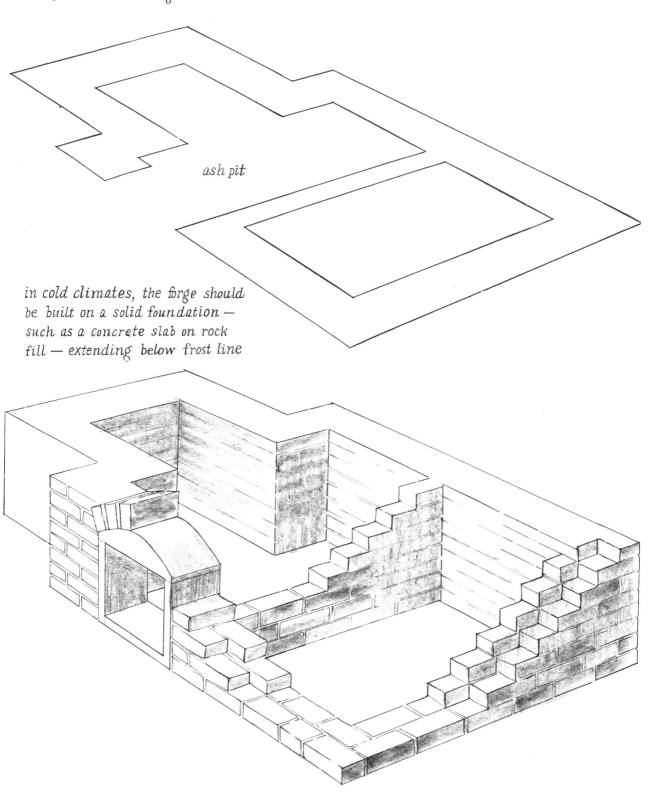

ash pit

in cold climates, the forge should be built on a solid foundation — such as a concrete slab on rock fill — extending below frost line

top. From checking the drawing, it appears that the base of the arch rests on the sixth course up; which in turn means it is time to form the arch. Knowing the treachery of human nature, imagine how easy it is to keep on laying up brick—the seventh course, the eighth course— and then suddenly see the mistake. A good move is to build a wooden form and set it in place as the very *first* course is laid. That way there is no forgetting. The same holds for that handy recess for storing a box of flux. Set the form on the wall and leave it there while you lay up course after course. Just having to move it will act as a reminder.

Bricklaying is an ancient trade involving specialized skills, the grasp of some engineering principles, and not a little art. It would be folly to think that anyone undertaking a brick forge for the first time will soon become an expert mason, which is not to say the attempt shouldn't be made. A considerable mass of useful information about masonry

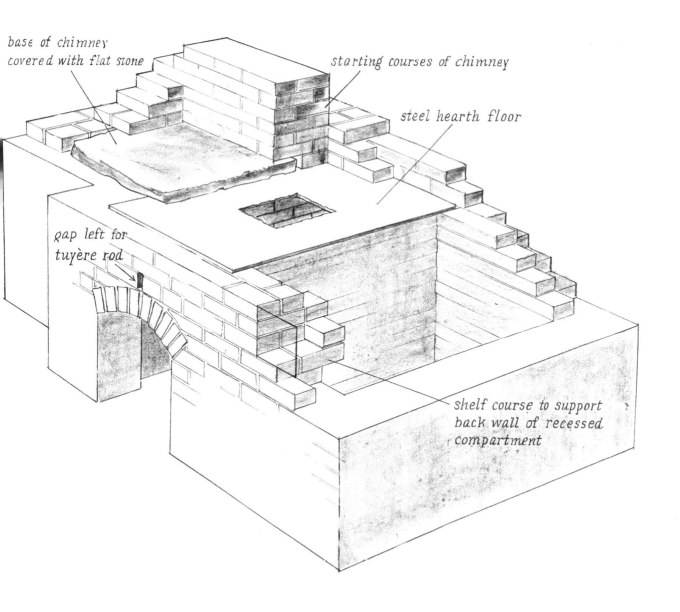

base of chimney covered with flat stone

starting courses of chimney

steel hearth floor

gap left for tuyère rod

shelf course to support back wall of recessed compartment

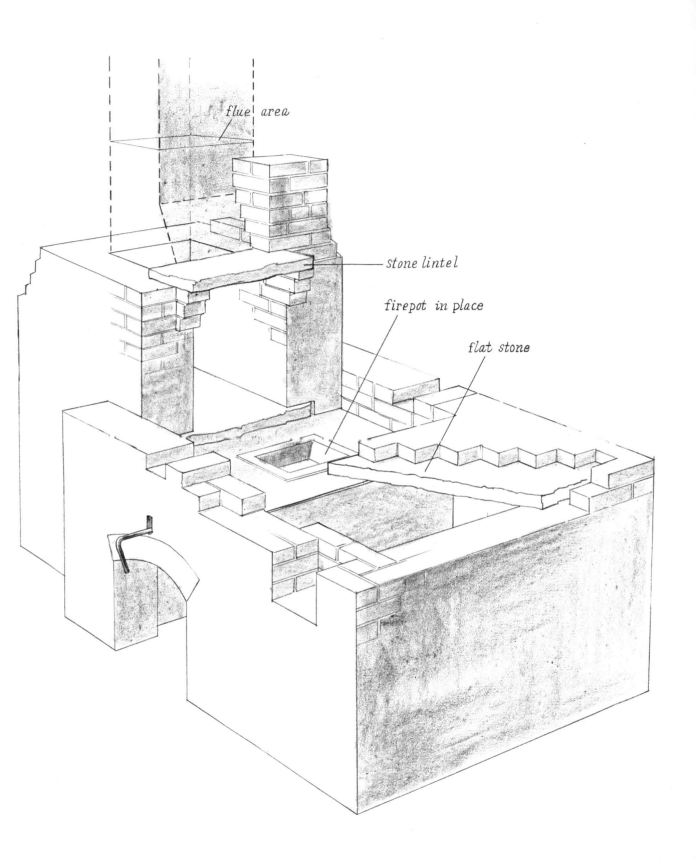

flue area

stone lintel

firepot in place

flat stone

can be found in books, some of it rather important to look into before mixing any mortar. The structural advantages of one bricklaying pattern over another, the function of staggered joints, and how to make a workmanlike corner on a wall are a few examples of the technology, an understanding of which will make the job come out better, and add zest to the work.

When the brickwork actually begins, with some normal fear and trepidation, the first courses can be started on the back side of the forge where the errors of inexperience won't show. By the time it comes around to doing the front, the workmanship should have grown a little more presentable.

Building a Leather Lung Bellows

The kind of bellows used in the 1800s is a machine that a man can build for himself. It is made of wood and leather, which can be obtained without a great deal of trouble, and is fashioned with a few hand tools. It uses no electricity, costs nothing to operate, and can be repaired without special equipment or the services of an expensive mechanic.

Some blacksmiths may object to the slower air stream, yet others may find it better suited to their work than a great blast from a motor-driven blower. Deciding to build a bellows instead of buying a blower is probably a matter of native ability and inclination: the man who wants to is often the one who can, and he goes ahead.

The construction of this bellows is essentially simple: Three pear-shaped wooden paddles around whose edges are fastened sections of leather to make a diaphragm, or lung, and two floating ribs whose purpose is to support and control the flexing of the leather sides.

Splined joints are used to join the planks in each solid paddle to achieve airtight conditions in the two chambers. Wood expands and contracts according to atmospheric conditions, and the splined joints allow the wood to "come and go" while maintaining tight joints. The lower chamber is the compression chamber, and the upper one the exhaust chamber, permitting air to escape through a duct cut in the nozzle end.

The bellows described here is a two-chamber machine, and an improvement over the single chamber type that produces an alternating air blast—that is, a rush of air followed by a dead pause while the

wooden framework of a double chamber bellows

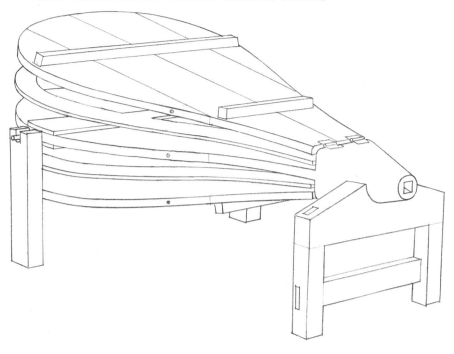

bellows sucks in new air to expel, and then another rush of expelled air. The double chamber bellows to a large extent overcomes the disadvantage of this "huff-and-puff" action. As the pole lever operates the bellows, the lower chamber compresses, forcing air through the valves into the upper chamber. The weight of a stone on the upper paddle presses down. By this action, the valves are closed, the air is trapped and can escape only through the nozzle into the blowpipe. While this is happening, another stroke of the overhead pole lever forces more air into the upper chamber. In effect, the two chambers are compressing air faster than the nozzle can exhaust it. This build–up tends to produce a steady stream of air. And, because the combined area of the two valves is much greater than that of the nozzle, it is not difficult to maintain a reserve of air. The bellows is really a compressed air pump that discharges or meters air through the funnel end.

The middle paddle should be made first and the nozzle woodwork attached to it. This unit is the spine of the machine. It is mounted stationary as a solid support for the moving parts—upper and lower paddles and floating ribs. Note that in making a pattern for the middle paddle, the full length of the plan on page 131 is used: five feet, seven and a half inches. The other paddles and floating ribs of course extend only as far as the back end of the nozzle. When this paddle and woodwork are completed, the iron drift pins can be put in, and the support frame

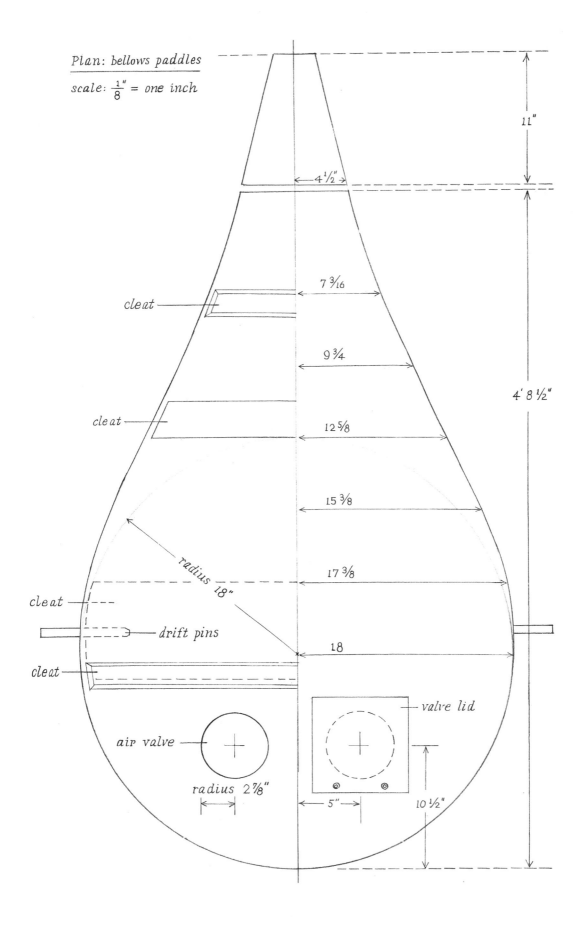

Plan: bellows paddles

scale: $\frac{1}{8}'' =$ one inch

11"

4½"

cleat

7 ³⁄₁₆

9 ¾

cleat

12 ⁵⁄₈

15 ³⁄₈

radius 18"

4' 8 ½"

17 ³⁄₈

cleat

drift pins

18

cleat

valve lid

air valve

radius 2⅞"

5"

10 ½"

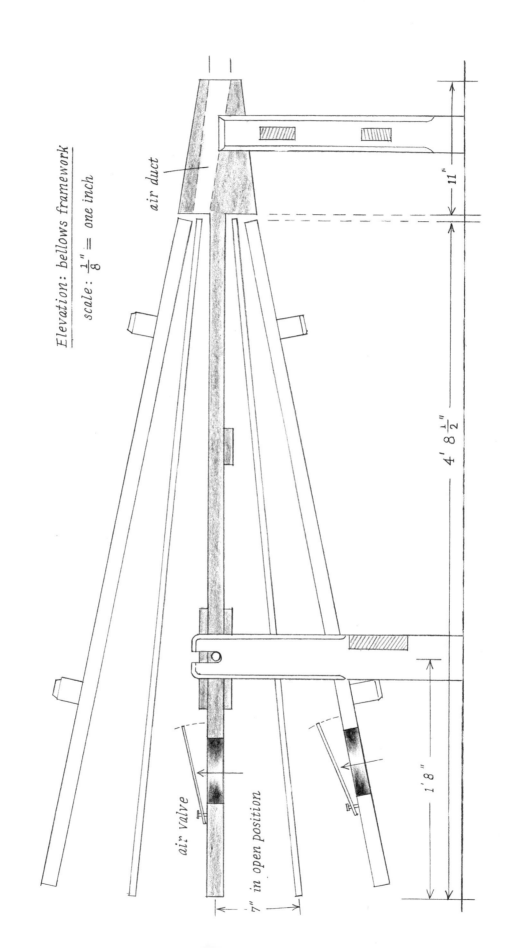

Elevation: bellows framework

scale: $\frac{1}{8}'' =$ one inch

air duct

air valve

7" in open position

1' 8"

4' 8 $\frac{1}{2}$"

11"

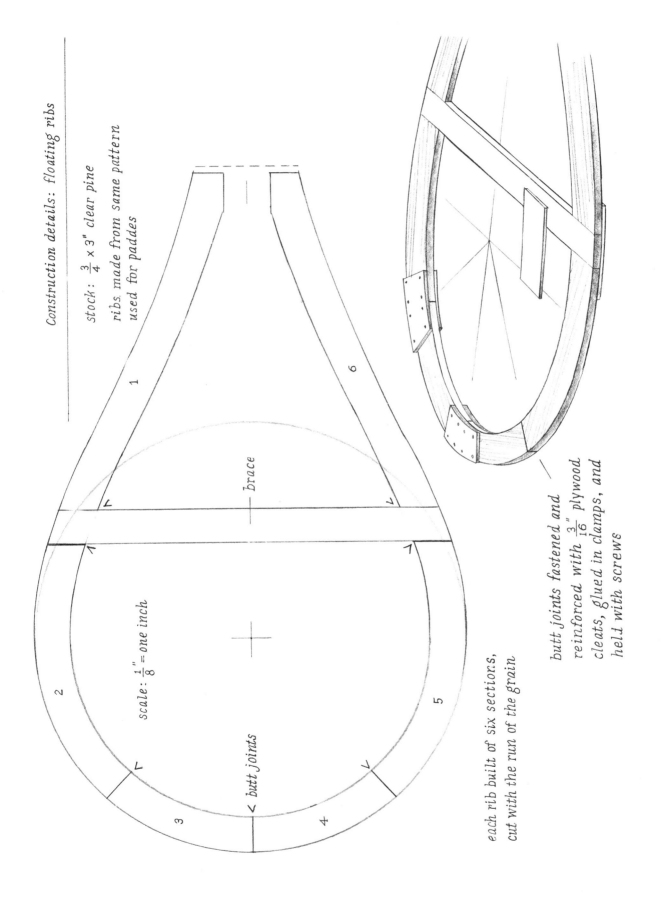

Construction details: floating ribs

stock: $\frac{3}{4}$ × 3" clear pine

ribs made from same pattern
used for paddes

1

6

brace

scale: $\frac{1}{8}$" = one inch

2

5

3

4

< butt joints

each rib built of six sections,
cut with the run of the grain

butt joints fastened and
reinforced with $\frac{3}{16}$" plywood
cleats, glued in clamps, and
held with screws

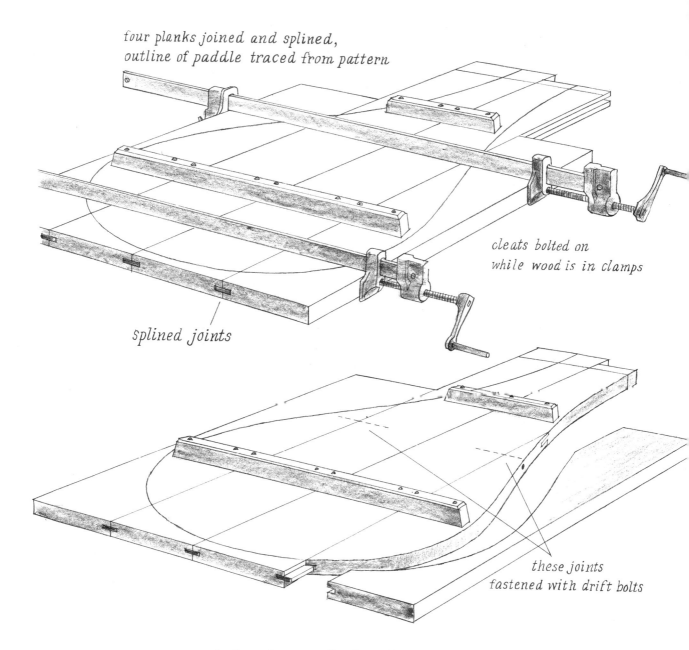

four planks joined and splined,
outline of paddle traced from pattern

cleats bolted on
while wood is in clamps

splined joints

these joints
fastened with drift bolts

built and set up. In determining the inside width of the rear support frame, allow at least an inch and a half clearance between the sides of the paddles and the upright posts of the frame. This leaves room to tack on the leather around the drift bolts, as well as space to accommodate the wood clamp strips. In these cramped quarters, some of the tacks and nails may have to be set with a nail punch.

At this point—before the other paddles or ribs are attached—hang the middle paddle in the support frame. It is much easier to carry on the rest of the construction when it is in a good solid position. Hang the

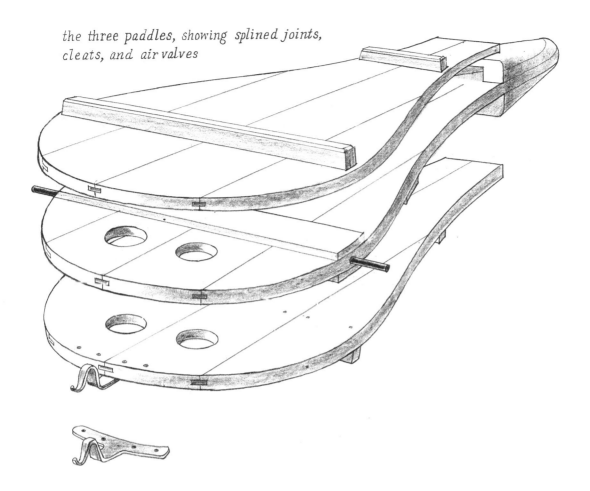

the three paddles, showing splined joints, cleats, and air valves

middle paddle upside down, so that the lower rib and lower paddle can be worked on without crawling under the frame. When these two parts have been attached, then the whole thing can be turned right side up, and the remaining work done.

The air valves, hinges, and their attachment to the two paddles (middle and lower) should be worked out carefully, as they are located inside the bellows, behind the leather sides.

The weight of the valves and the ease with which they open and close are critical to the operation of the machine. The valve lids must be light enough so the in-rushing air will lift them, and heavy enough to drop in place over the valve holes once air has been admitted. The question of what is heavy enough is answered best by trial and error, of course, before the valves are built and installed—and then closed in.

Make the lids large enough to cover the circular hole with about an inch and a quarter to spare. The lid should be thin, light in weight and of a stable material not likely to warp. A good lid can be made of $\frac{3}{16}$-inch clear pine, reinforced with a pair of thin hardwood cleats

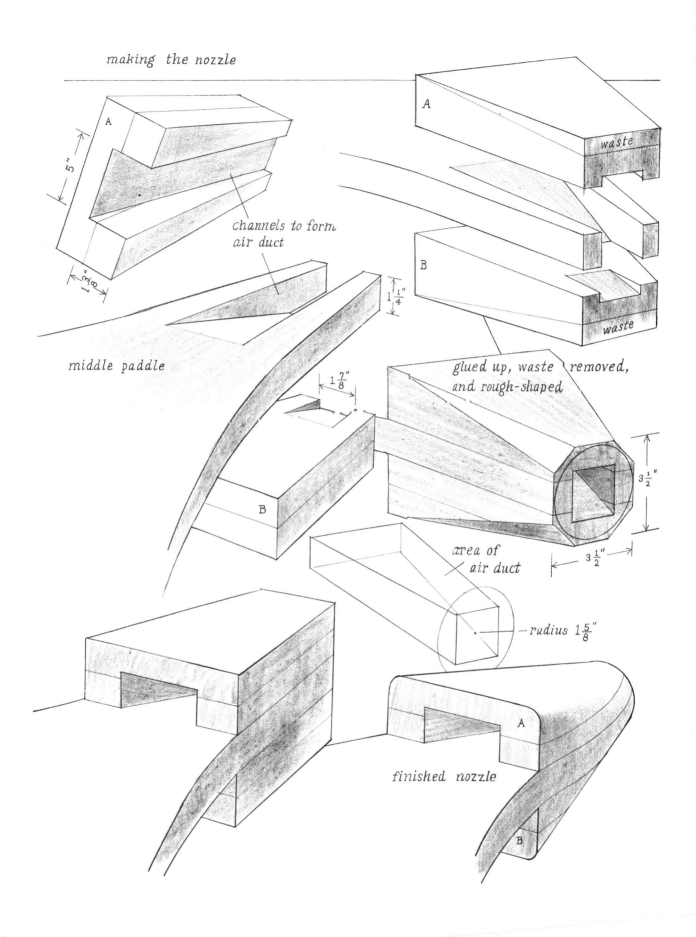

making the nozzle

A

5"

1 3/8"

channels to form
air duct

middle paddle

1 1/4"

A

waste

B

waste

1 7/8"

B

glued up, waste removed,
and rough-shaped

3 1/2"

3 1/2"

area of
air duct

radius 1 5/8"

A

B

finished nozzle

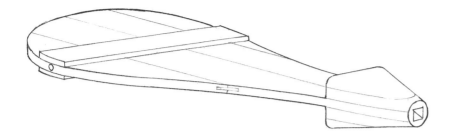

glued to the top to control warping. An alternative might be plywood, provided it is not too heavy.

The lid will make a more nearly airtight seal against the hole if the underside is padded in the manner of a flute valve. A piece of chamois leather, felt, or cotton fabric will work. Cut the material slightly smaller than the lid, and attach it to the underside of the lid with a thin border of glue around the edges only, leaving the center portion of material loose, which will act as a cushion.

The valves described here have no hinges as such, but are mounted over wood dowels projecting through holes in the valve lid. These dowel holes should be somewhat larger than the dowels, and elongated to allow the lid to swing up. The elongation runs parallel with the center line of the bellows. This makes a free-floating valve cover that pops up and seats more readily than one hinged with metal hinges, which get sticky and rusty. A couple of trial dowel pins set into a scrap of wood are useful in enlarging the holes and trying out the action, which can be further tested as follows:

Find a hardcover book with covers measuring at least 8 inches x 10 inches. Lay the book flat on a table. Just catch the tip of a finger under the edge of the book cover and raise it three or four inches. Then let it fall. The bellows valve should work just as easily as that. If it doesn't, and the lid drops with an audible "clunk," it is probably too heavy, and a lighter version will have to be tried. If, on the other hand, it drops with scarcely a whisper, it may be too light. The valve lid should strike the hole with an action positive enough to seat and seal in the air. Small weights—a scrap of sheet lead, or a nut—can be attached to the lid to adjust the action.

Although the object is to make the bellows as nearly airtight as possible, literal perfection is out of the question. More than likely there will be some leaks, but this will not materially affect the function of the bellows. The valves on some of the small fireplace bellows were nothing more than squares of cloth tacked over the valve hole, yet because of the rapidity of the pumping motion, air leakage was not a problem.

137

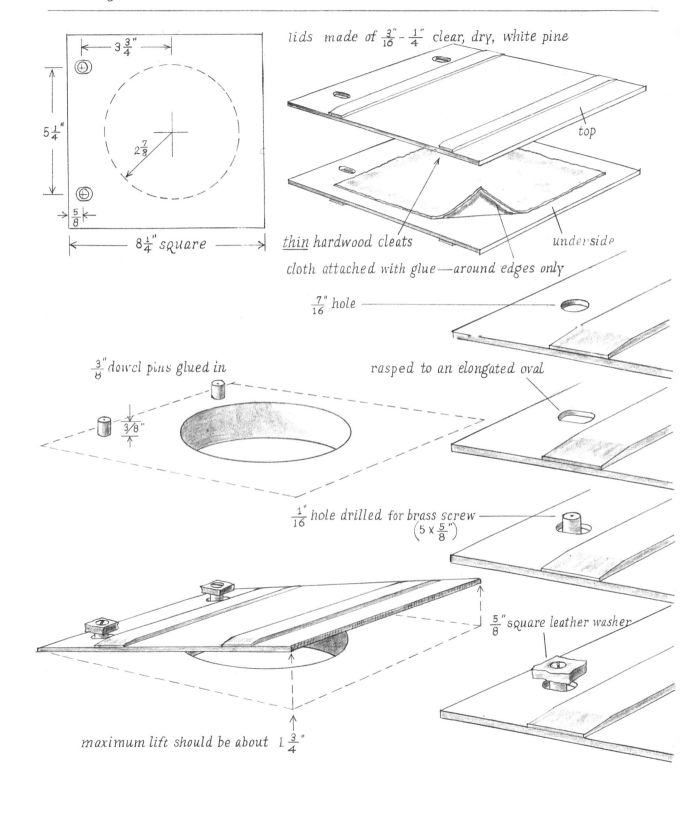

$3\frac{3}{4}"$

$5\frac{1}{4}"$

$2\frac{7}{8}$

$\frac{5}{8}$

$8\frac{1}{4}"$ square

lids made of $\frac{3}{16}" - \frac{1}{4}"$ *clear, dry, white pine*

top

underside

thin hardwood cleats

cloth attached with glue — around edges only

$\frac{7}{16}"$ hole

$\frac{3}{8}"$ dowel pins glued in

$\frac{3}{8}"$

rasped to an elongated oval

$\frac{1}{16}"$ hole drilled for brass screw
$\left(5 \times \frac{5}{8}"\right)$

$\frac{5}{8}"$ square leather washer

maximum lift should be about $1\frac{3}{4}"$

A final test of the valves can be made after the leather has been tacked on, but *before* the wood clamp strips have been nailed on. If any modifications are indicated at this stage, only the back section of leather will have to be taken off.

When the upper and lower paddles, floating ribs, and air valves have been made, the work of assembling all the parts can proceed. Because of the cramped space where the paddles and ribs are attached to the nozzle end, the floating ribs should be attached first, and the upper and lower paddles last. With all four moving parts attached to the middle paddle (two upper and two lower), make a quick check to see that all the hinges work easily and aren't pinching or straining the screws. Then nail a pair of scantlings across the back end of the bellows, spacing the paddles and ribs seven inches on centers. This is the maximum amount of expansion of the lung; and this will also keep everything in proper alignment while the leather is put on.

When leather is forced into sharp creases and repeatedly flexed at the same places, it tends to crack and develop air leaks, especially as it ages and dries out. In the case of a small fireplace bellows no bigger than sixteen inches long, this is not a serious consideration, since the expanse of leather—the distance between the two paddles—is small and the amount of flexing and folding relatively slight.

On a large bellows such as this one, however, the expanse of leather from one paddle to the next is considerably greater—about 14 inches across the back end—and must have some additional support. The floating ribs are necessary to control where and how much the leather folds, creases, and flexes as the bellows "breathes."

attaching paddles to nozzle

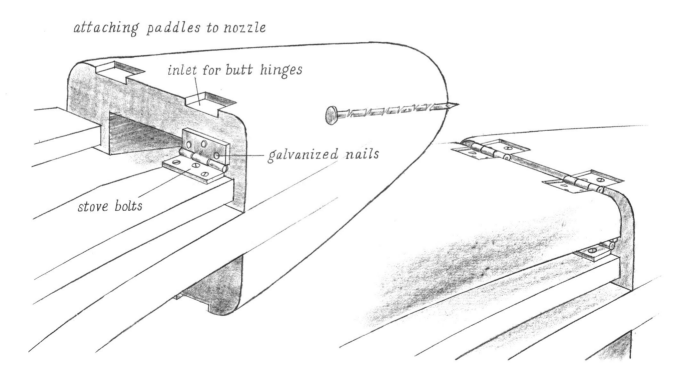

inlet for butt hinges

galvanized nails

stove bolts

the completed woodwork, ready for attachment of the leather

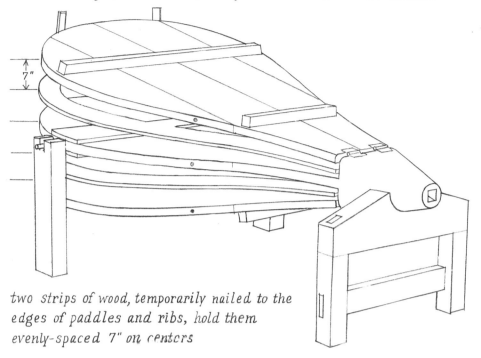

two strips of wood, temporarily nailed to the edges of paddles and ribs, hold them evenly-spaced 7" on centers

Leather can usually be obtained from people whose business depends on it: manufacturers of shoes, handbags, harness, saddle bags and other horse equipment, and tanners. Whole skins or large pieces are the most economical, as fewer seams will be required, and consequently fewer places where air leaks can develop.

The gauge, or thickness, is important. Thin leather works easiest and flexes without any severe strain, but will not last as long as heavier material. Although thin stuff is adequate for a fireplace bellows, the forge bellows needs something with more tensile strength, because most of the weight of the lower paddle, for example, is suspended by the leather sides. The heavy leather used in chair seats represents the other extreme—too thick and stiff to bend at all. And even if it could bend, cracks would break out in a very short time. A practical compromise is leather approximately $\frac{3}{32}$ of an inch thick, with enough "body" and at the same time good flexibility. Supple is the word, and a characteristic that can be determined from flexing and rolling it in the hands.

The leather should be treated—particularly on the flesh side—before it is attached to the wood frame. Otherwise, it is impossible to get at. The outside, or hair side, can of course be treated at any time, and should periodically be lubricated as needed. Use neatsfoot oil or one of the modern leather lubricants that has a preservative ingredient. This treatment should be done when the leather is fresh, while the pores are open and receptive to a good soaking. Once the pores have begun to clog with soot, dirt, and dust—all of which abound in a blacksmith shop—it is hard to soften up leather. Bearing in mind that the flesh side will be out of reach, it is advisable to give it two applications (with a drying-in interval between) before it is cut and fitted, and possibly a third application after the pieces have been sewn together, just prior to nailing it in place.

If a large enough hide could be found, of the right thickness, the leather conceivably could be put on in one big piece. Yet a much better "tailoring" job can be done by stitching together smaller pieces, especially as some fullness must be allowed at the nozzle end and over the hinges.

The safest method is to make a complete paper pattern from which to cut and piece the leather. The patterns in the illustration are in two half sections, each one made up of six pieces. The two halves are lapped and nailed on the edges of the middle paddle. If the valves should give trouble later on, the leather panels 1 and 2 can be opened up without having to take the whole lung apart. The wood clamp strips for these two sections are nailed on as separate pieces.

The largest pieces of leather, requiring the least number of seams, should be used on the back end of the bellows where the most flexing takes place. A seam of two thicknesses of leather, cemented and sewn,

making paper patterns for the leather sides

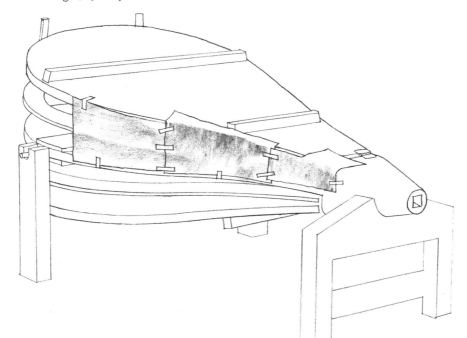

141

the finished patterns

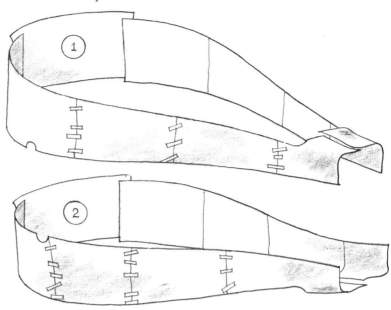

tacking on the leather

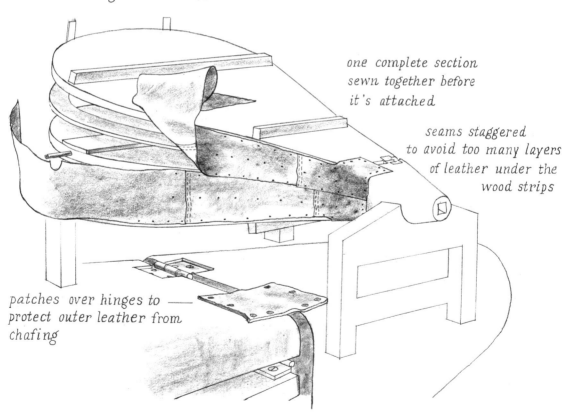

one complete section
sewn together before
it's attached

seams staggered
to avoid too many layers
of leather under the
wood strips

patches over hinges to ———
protect outer leather from
chafing

will not flex as easily as free leather. This is not a serious drawback toward the nozzle end, where the flexing is minimal. In most of the old bellows, the seams were simply double-sewn without any adhesive, but a much tighter seam can be made by using a liquid fabric cement or shoemaker's cement applied to both surfaces before .sewing. A hand stitching awl—the variety with a bobbin inside the handle—works very well. Use a good stout shoemaker's or harnessmaker's thread, and before loading up the bobbin, draw the thread several times across a chunk of beeswax to give it a rot-resisting coating.

It is not necessary to sandpaper the edges of the paddles before nailing on the leather. A few passes with a plane or a spokeshave will leave a good clean seat for the leather. The leather sides are attached in two stages. In the first, the leather is tacked in place so that it lies naturally without diagonal stress puckers, and with some fullness at the hinges around the nozzle end. Use large carpet tacks with flat heads, spacing them about three or four inches apart, so that as adjustments are needed, there won't be dozens of tacks to remove. This step can be compared to the process, in sewing, of basting the pieces of material together before doing the final stitching.

Where the leather touches wood, avoid any humps between tacks. These bulges can never be drawn down flat, even under the pressure of the clamp strips, and they will leak. On the other hand, it is just as important not to stretch the leather to make it lie flat. Just set it so that it lies smooth and flat on its own.

Once the leather is smooth and flat, the second stage can proceed: nailing wooden clamp strips over the leather, clear round the edges of all paddles and ribs. These strips squeeze the leather into continuous contact with the wood. Without them, the spaces between tacks— even if the number of tacks was doubled—would belly up and create dozens of air leaks.

It's a good precaution, again remembering that the vital parts will be inaccessible, to try out the action of the bellows before nailing on the wood clamp strips. Once the leather sides are all tacked on, the lower and upper paddles can be worked up and down to see that the leather is smoothly attached and is not puckering in a way to strain or damage it. This test also provides a chance to check the operation of the air valves. Hold the palm of a hand tight against the nozzle while someone operates the bellows. A fair estimate of air pressure can be made this way.

Clamp-strips ½-inch square can be sawn out of oak or white ash. Both these woods take well to steam-bending, which is recommended to get the best seam around the curved parts of the paddles, as well as the one that circles the nozzle end.

Box nails about 1½ inches long will hold the strips firm, as they will reach well into the wood. Space the nails about every inch and a half, and plan on drilling holes for the nails: both ash and oak are easily split.

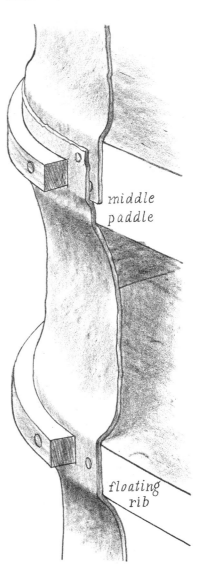

nailing strips over seams in leather

middle paddle

floating rib

143

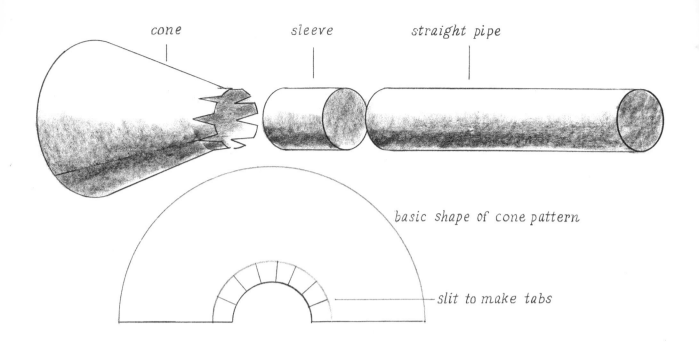

cone   sleeve   straight pipe

basic shape of cone pattern

slit to make tabs

The sheet metal work consists of three sections: a cone that fits over the bellows nozzle and tapers to the diameter of the blowpipe; a short sleeve to connect the cone to the blowpipe; and a straight section (the blowpipe) connecting to the firepot. The diameter of the blowpipe is determined by the inside diameter of the air intake sleeve on the firepot. The blowpipe fits inside this sleeve, and when finally assembled, can be sealed with furnace cement to make it airtight.

Paper patterns for these components will save time and anguish. Be sure to allow at least an extra inch and a half for each of the slip joints, and a half inch for all seams that are to be fastened and soldered.

The joints in these three sections are fastened with sheet metal screws and solder. Save the soldering until the last: after making all the sections, try them out for snug fit before doing any soldering. When assembled, the end of the cone section slips inside the blowpipe, and the blowpipe inside the firepot sleeve. These slip joints should stay tight without any fastening, but sheet metal screws can be inserted if needed.

Making and hanging the pole lever is the final step in building the bellows. Cut a good straight pine pole, skin off the bark, and smooth off any knots. The pole must be long enough to reach from the back end of the bellows to a point within an easy arm's reach of where the blacksmith stands at the forge. There is no formula for determining the precise length. Since it's easier to cut off a pole than to go back to the woods for another, cut one that is considerably longer than required, and work out the details by trial and error.

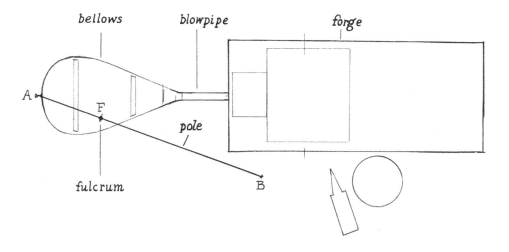

In the diagram, the pole is shown as line A-B, with the fulcrum (F) somewhere in between. Notice that the fulcrum here is offset from the center line of the bellows, in order to dodge the stack and bring the end of the pole close to the anvil. The exact location of F can best be determined by trying it out. Rig a temporary hanger for F, and a temporary lift rope at A. The hanger can be shifted and adjusted as needed.

The pole should balance with sufficient weight on the B end to take up any slack in the lift, or to just barely begin to lift the bellows— but no more. In other words, it should all be nicely arranged so that when the hand grabs the pole to lift, the pole should *lift*, with no motion wasted in taking up slack.

Finding the correct distance between A and F will also require some experimentation. The maximum allowable lift at the back of the bellows is only about five or six inches. If the distance A-F is too great, there will be more lift than necessary, but there will also be more elbow grease needed to do the lifting.

When all this preliminary trial and error is done, the permanent hanger and other linkage can be made and installed.

A chain or rope should be rigged over the back end of the bellows and attached to a hook in the upper paddle. This keeps the paddle from compressing too far and causing unnecessary folding of the leather. It also provides a way to hook the paddle in a raised position if the bellows is to be out of use for any length of time. Leaving the leather in a compressed fixed position will increase the chances for cracks and leaks to develop. For this same reason, the lower paddle should be blocked up when not in use, to take the strain off the leather.

Presumably everything is done: the forge, stack, and now the bellows. Not a little work has gone into putting together this old-time equipment, and now the moment of truth is at hand. When the forge

hanging the pole

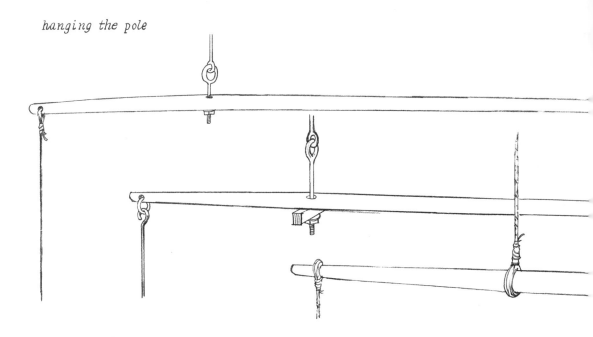

is fired up and you grab that pole for the first time, comes the dreadful question: Will it work? Did I remember to lay a good stone on top of the bellows? Perhaps there is some long-forgotten initiation rite with which to begin operation of a new forge, something comparable to a housewarming, or nailing a rooftree to a newly framed building. Well, if there isn't there should be. Any proud father of a strange contraption like this who has come this far—made plans, scale drawings, calculations, and trials at every step of the way—surely has the imagination, the wit, and the reverence to contrive a ceremony suitable to the baptism of his fiery creation.

Epilogue

12

By the turn of the century, blacksmithing had begun a sharp descent on the incline to virtual extinction. The gasoline engine and the proliferation of new developments in the iron and steel industry were creating changes of such a radical nature that in the brief period from 1900 to 1930 innovations in manufacturing, transportation, and communication would make nearly obsolete not only the blacksmith and his work but also the kinds of articles that had been in demand during the simpler life of the nineteenth century.

One of the first factors that contributed to the eventual decline and disappearance of the village blacksmith's craft was the rise of the factory system. Iron manufacturing in quantity, stimulated by the invention of thousands of mechanical devices and tools, soon began to turn out factory products that were easily obtained and replaced, and that were priced below the smith's ability to compete. Nor could he possibly have duplicated with his simple forge and anvil the incessant variety of the new, ingenious articles of every description that the factories provided.

Then, in 1875, with Sidney G. Thomas's perfection of Henry Bessemer's revolutionary steel process—already profitably in use by its discoverer since 1856—the Age of Steel was born. A whole new development in metals, supported by new discoveries in the physical sciences—especially in chemistry—came into being. Steel, once too expensive for anything but luxury items, could at last be made from almost any kind of iron. With steel undisputed king, the demand for wrought iron and for the blacksmith's art—always excepting the need for horseshoes—

dwindled to an extent that proved disastrous to the business of the village smith.

Even before the emergence of iron factories and their metamorphosis into the gigantic iron and steel manufacturing complex of the following decades, the blacksmith had been increasingly hampered by the growing use of coal and its derivative fuel, coke. These had been found to be more economical for commercial ironmaking. The coal industry grew and fed the furnaces of the expanding ironmaking industry, which, in turn, poured increasing supplies of iron into the growing iron manufacturing industry.

In the late nineteenth century, inventions, scientific discoveries of every sort and variety, and the onrush of modern industrial methods began to mechanize, enrich, and reshape America, to empty the farms, modernize the villages, and crowd the cities. The age of the automobile and of electrical wonders was at hand. In a new culture, with new standards of living and an accelerated pace of existence, wrought iron was wholly inadequate, as is implied in the following chronological list of events.

CHRONOLOGICAL LIST OF EVENTS
IN THE INDUSTRIAL EXPANSION OF THE UNITED STATES:
1885–1910

1886   Endless-chain tractor invented by Charles Dinsmoor, of Warren, Pennsylvania.

       Keyboard typesetting machine, of the type invented in 1884 by Otto Mergenthaler, installed in the *New York Tribune* plant.

       Electric welding process invented by Elihu Thompson, of Lynn, Massachusetts.

1887   Quadruple newspaper printing press built by R. Hoe & Company, New York, for the *New York World* plant. It produced an eight-page newspaper, printed, folded, and cut, ready for delivery, at the rate of 48,000 an hour.

1888   George Eastman, of Rochester, New York, began manufacturing the Kodak No. 1, a box camera that used roll film.

1889   Jones & Laughlin, of Pittsburgh, Pennsylvania, produced the first steel I beams made of Bessemer steel.

1892   Acetylene, or carbide gas, made by Thomas Leopold Willson, of the Willson Aluminum Company of Spray, North Carolina. Later manufactured on a commercial scale and used in welding.

148

1893   Brick-paved rural road begun on the Wooster (Ohio) Pike. Now known as U.S. 42, it was eight feet wide, laid on a base of broken stone, and edged with stone curbing.

Henry Ford road-tested his first gasoline-powered automobile.

1894   Manganese-steel railroad track manufactured by William Wharton, Jr. and Company, Inc., High Bridge, New Jersey.

1900   Survey figures showed there were fewer than 8000 automobiles in the United States, and less than 10 miles of concrete paved roads.

First quantity-production automobile factory established; the Olds Company in Detroit, Michigan, manufactured 400 cars the first year, 1600 the second year, and 4000 the third.

1902   International Harvester Company incorporated in New Jersey. One of the largest manufacturers of farm machinery now in existence, in 1902 it controlled 85 per cent of farm machine production.

1904   Automobile tire chains invented by Harry D. Weed, of Canastota, New York. Weed's patent was eventually acquired by the American Chain and Cable Company.

1906   The Pennsylvania Railroad announced that all its coaches would henceforth be made of steel, and their wooden coaches discarded.

1907   First automobile with left-hand steering, the "Northern," built by the Northern Motor Car Company, of Detroit, Michigan.

1908   Henry Ford introduced his Model T Ford.

1909   Henry Ford built 19,051 Model T cars.

1910   First completely self-contained washing machine, the "Thor," manufactured by the Hurley Machine Company, Chicago, Illinois.

Typical of many blacksmiths in old New England was Albert F. Whitney, of Hartsville, Massachusetts, who first opened his forge for business in 1885.* Of his three sons, one—Raymond—took a particular interest in blacksmithing and learned the trade. By the time Raymond was serving in the army in World War I, he had also discovered

---

* Father and son, the Whitneys carried on the blacksmithing business for about fifty-five years.

149

another absorbing interest—automobiles. Symbolic of the adjustment from one trade to another, and prophetic of things to come, the following paraphrase of Raymond Whitney's description of the years between 1890 and 1910 in part describes in personal terms the decline of blacksmithing:

> I started working [in the smithy] when I was still a kid going to school, working before school and again when I got home. The first job I had was shoeing horses—the kickers. I got all of them to shoe. We had a big sling with a canvas girth that went under the horse's belly, and when it was tightened up, it raised the horse so his feet were just touching the floor.
>
> We shoed horses from almost every town within a fifty mile radius—Pittsfield, Lee, Tyringham, Lennox, and from some of the towns in Connecticut like Norfolk and Winsted. They'd bring horses up in a truck and take them back the same way. There were three blacksmiths in the shop then, that is two besides my father [Albert F.]. All the old shoes were thrown outside on a pile. Over the years that pile grew and grew. When I finally sold it, there were 55 tons of iron in it. We had several men who guessed beforehand how many tons there were, and my guess was the closest.
>
> We bought horseshoe nails forty boxes at a time, and shoes in kegs. We generally got forty to fifty kegs of shoes at once, each keg weighing about 112 pounds. All of our iron came by railroad [Berkshire Division of the New Haven], and we had to truck it out here by horse and wagon. It was unloaded in Great Barrington [8 miles].
>
> We ran another shop at the same time in Marlboro, which we worked on Tuesdays and Fridays. The going wage then was twenty cents an hour. That was about the time [approx. 1912] I got interested in automobiles. An old Zeitz truck going through town broke down and was towed into the yard by the blacksmith shop. I would go and look at it, and one day my father asked me if I was going to fix it. I said I thought I could do the job. I had looked it over quite a few times. He said that if I thought I could repair it, he would speak to the man that owned it and he believed he could get me the job.
>
> I don't know how many hours I spent on that old truck. I tore the engine apart and worked for weeks and weeks, and when it was done I got paid $480. The truck ran for several years after that without a breakdown.

The son carried over his training at his father's forge into the business of becoming an auto mechanic. He studied books on automobile mechanics at night, and worked out his apprenticeship on the cars that were brought in. If no parts were to be had—and interchangeable parts had not yet made it to the Montgomery Ward catalog—then young Whitney made them in the blacksmith shop. As the years went by, the garage grew larger and the smithy was in less demand. Though the garage was back in the Berkshire Hills, the new mechanic's reputation reached as far away as New York City. It was then the custom among people who could afford cars to "put them up" for the winter, and many a Packard or Cadillac spent the winter on blocks in the Whitney garage while its innards were restored to top condition.

Even when they began to look more like cars and less like buggies, the new contraptions were cumbersome and unreliable—they wouldn't run long without a mishap. And they were expensive. In 1900, an average automobile cost about $3,500, which put it in a class that only royalty and the wealthy could afford. Yet within a decade the Model T Ford could be bought new for $360, or secondhand for around $25. Farmers were quick to see the usefulness of the new machines. In them they could get to town and back without taking the whole day away from farm work, and the family could venture forth to visit relatives who lived as far away as fifty or sixty miles. As the automobile rapidly outgrew the novelty stage, the horse was relegated pretty much to the farm, where he carried on as before with agricultural chores. When cars took over the roads, the blacksmith's work dropped off still more. Buggies, wagons, and carriages began collecting cobwebs in the sheds, yielding first place to the sleds and log scoots that were still needed for gathering wood in wintertime. For a brief period each year, the heavy snowfalls brought the blacksmith back to full activity, for marvelous as it was, the automobile could not buck through a New England winter.

Nevertheless, the blacksmith, for all practical purposes, has vanished. The farrier, however, remains—to shoe saddle horses and race horses, whose numbers have maintained a steady level. The persistent popularity of horseback riding, fox hunting, harness and thoroughbred racing, bulwarked by a tremendously increased number of horse shows, has assured the farrier's future—at least as far as can now be seen.

But the farrier of today is no more like the village blacksmith than a cart horse is like a trotter. He is a businessman who uses modern accounting methods. He has no blacksmith shop, having been forced by circumstances to take to the road as an itinerant expert. His customers are scattered too far afield; no longer do they take the horse to the smith. Instead, he makes his appointments by telephone, grouping the calls to make the most efficient use of his time, since he often drives seventy-five to a hundred miles a day. His "smithy" is a pickup truck that carries a small hand-blower forge, a keg or two of horseshoes, a box of horsenails, toolbox, leather apron, and a bag of fuel. He sets shoes cold, using the forge only to fit the iron to the hoof. In his busy schedule—often arranged weeks in advance—there is no time for gossip or horse-trading as he works. He must work steadily, collect his twelve or fifteen dollars, and move on to the next place, after loading his equipment back into the truck. In a good day he may make something like $135, yet his expenses are far greater than were those of his colonial predecessor.

Along with the demand for the articles the blacksmith once made, the smells, the sounds, and the mysterious excitement of the forge have vanished. Though there are still a few men who know the old skills, the magnitude of the blacksmith's place in the larger order of society has evaporated, for technology has supplanted the handicraftsman. Writing in *Fincher's Trade Reviews* in 1864, a contributor envisioned just such a change when he said of the shoe industry what could as well have been applied to blacksmithing:

> The little shoemaker's shop and bench are passing rapidly away, soon to be known no more among us, and the immense factory, with its laboring steam engine and its busy hum of whirling wheels, is rising up in their place, to change the whole face of things in the ancient and honored metropolis of workers in the gentle craft of leather.

The blacksmith flourished as a major social force in the modern world for more than two thousand years. During forty generations of hand labor there had been scarcely a single significant change in his tools and anvil techniques, or in the smelting, forging, and treatment of iron. Then—nearly within the span of one lifetime—the vital role of the blacksmith vanished.

Appendix

Charcoal burning persisted in parts of New England as late as the 1920s, supplying fuel not only for the blacksmith but for many homes as well. The process was as ancient as iron smelting itself, and the selection of a site for the iron furnace included finding a satisfactory stand of timber for the purpose. So great was the demand by ironworks for charcoal fuel that dangerous inroads were made on timber stands all up and down the eastern seaboard. The following quotation from the *Pennsylvania Gazette* for October 4, 1770, will give some idea of the sheer volume of timber that was stripped off the land to feed a typical ironworks:

To be LETT for a Term of YEARS

Andover Furnace, situate in the County of Sussex, in West New-Jersey, on a Branch of Paquest River, together with an elegant Stone Dwelling-house, Stables, Smith's Shop, Springhouse, and a Number of Outhouses for Workmen; a large Coalhouse in which there is at least 7 Week's Stock of Coals for the next Blast; also 5000 acres of well timbered Land to accomodate the Furnace, ...*

The charcoal burner collected his stockpile of oak and ash—which were especially good for smelting fuel—during the winter months,

* From Charles S. Boyer, *Early Forges and Furnaces in New Jersey.*

charcoal burner's sod hut

when skidding it out to his yard was the easiest. When mild weather came, he cut the wood into short billets about two or three feet long, and sorted them according to thickness.

The stack of wood was built in an open clearing—often hacked out of a thickly wooded place. The sod was removed and set aside in a pile, and in the center of this skinned area a stake was driven into the ground for a center pole. Billets of wood were then leaned against the stake to make a tentlike core. More and more pieces were added—the thickest ones in the center and the smaller ones near the outside—until a mound had been built about the size of a beaver house. Short billets were laid flat on top of the pile, radiating from the center pole. The whole mound was covered over with the sod and a layer of dirt, damp earth, or wet green hay. The center stake was then removed, leaving a shaft into which hot charcoal was put to start the burning.

But the stacked wood was not to be allowed to *burn*: only a slow, permeating smoulder was needed to transform it by carbonization into a clean-burning fuel. The heat developed by the burning of a small amount of wood in the core served to char what remained. The burning process might take a week or two, depending on the size of the stack and the kind of wood used. All this time, the burner never left the pile.

> He [the burner] went once a year and took his food along and a cover to sleep under and did not come down until the fire was out.
> . . . With the sod he had dug up first he would cover the whole stack; this and the dirt he used kept the fire from breaking out into a blaze. . . . The slow heat charred the whole stack.*

Through a small peephole in the sod covering the burner watched his stack constantly, alert for the appearance of holes, which he covered at once with more wet dirt. When the stack was "done" to his satisfaction, it was allowed to cool and go out, or was doused all over with water.

* From Marion Nicholl Rawson, *Candle Days*.

155

TABLE 1

RESULTS OF A STUDY ON EXPANSION OF
HORSES' HOOFS

| | Number of Experiments | —Dilation in Millimeters— | | |
		At Outer Wall of Heel	At Inner Wall of Heel	Between
At rest	32	0.25	0.30	0.55
Walk	33	0.55	0.70	1.28
Trot	69	0.84	1.22	2.23
Gallop	12	1.06	1.81	3.04

SOURCE: Jno. A. W. Dollar, *A Handbook of Horseshoeing*. Dollar was also the author of a work titled *An Atlas of Veterinary Surgical Operations*. The above study, credited to one Lungwitz by Dollar, also revealed that the hoof is shortened from front to back when dilation takes place, and that a well-developed and untrimmed frog favored dilation at the points where the hoof was in contact with the ground.

TABLE 2

TEMPERING TEMPERATURES, COLOR OF SCALE, TYPES OF TOOLS

Degrees F.	Color	Tools
200		
375		Gauges
	Very pale yellow	
430		Light turning
440	Lemon yellow	Lathe, scrapers
460	Straw yellow	Drills, milling cutters
480	Dark straw	Punches, rock drills, shears
500	Brown	Woodworking, reamers, stone mason's
510	Brown with red spots	Wood chisels
520	Brown with purple spots	Sledge hammers
530	Light purple	Axes, adzes, hot sets, augers, blacksmith hammers
540	Full purple	
550	Dark purple	Cold chisels
560	Light blue	Screwdrivers, saws
570	Blue	
580	Dark blue	Wagon springs
610		
630	Blue tinged with green	

TABLE 3

BLACKSMITH'S DAILY RECORD FOR JANUARY, 1842

1	to repair sleigh	$ .13	Samuel Wells
	to repair caps pins	.06	Jon^{th.} Graves
	to toed & sett shoe & mend sleigh	.34	Leonard Graves
3	to make & cut 13 bolts	.33	Alfred Root
	to 4 blind hooks	.13	Josiah Hayden
	to toed sharp 4 shoes	.56	Wm. Jones
4	to make & cut 8 bolts	.20	Alfred Root
	to repair cutter	.33	Cyrus Miller
	to repair sleigh	1.33	Wm. Lewis
5	to toed & sharp 2 shoes	.56	Wm. Lewis
	to 2 rings & hooks & mend chain	.37	John Miller
	to 4 clasps & staples	.50	Ezekiel Eldridge
6	to make & cut 27 bolts	.68	Alfred Root
7	to strap on sled	.17	John Graves
	to 1 old ox shoe sett 1 & mend Staple	.25	Fred Moses
10	to toed & sharp 2 shoes	.50	Joel Hayden
	to mop iron	.34	Josiah Hayden
11	to cut & head 64 bolts	1.75	Alfred Root
12	to mend chain	.16	Leonard Dwight
	to toed & sett 2 shoes	.28	Chester Shelden
13	to use of plow	.75	Thad^s Bartlett
	to toed & sett 1 shoe	.14	John Miller
14	to toed 1 sharp 2 old shoes	.58	Wm. Loomis
	to mend chain	.06	John Graves
	to 2 new toed 2 shoes & mend chain	1.00	Spencer Graves
	to 2 hooks for chain	.20	Royal Fairfield
15	to 1 new link & mend chain	.17	Jon^{th.} Graves
17	to clasp & staple & mend cutter	.34	Alfred Root
	to mend chain	.08	John Graves
	to toed 2 & sharp 2 shoes	.56	Wm. Lewis
	to toed 2 sharp 2 shoes	.45	Presc^t Williams
18	to toed & sharp 4 shoes	.56	Josiah Hayden
19	to sharp & sett 3 shoes	.34	Thad Bartlett
	& mend chain	.08	
	to repair centre pin & 8 rivets & hoop	.63	Alfred Root
	to mend tongs	.17	Josiah Hayden
20	to shg oxen & mend chain	.42	Royal Fairfield
24	to toed 2 sharp 2 shoes	.56	Sam¹ Wells
	to shg oxen	1.00	Cyrus Miller

25	to repair whifeltree	.10	Spencer Root
26	to toed 1 sharp 3 shoes	.50	Thad Bartlett
	to 2 hooks & staples	.17	Alfred Root
	to 10 hooks & staples	.67	
	to 24 lbs cast iron	.24	
	to shg oxen new	2.00	Leonard Dwight
	to mend waggon	.42	Sam¹ Wells
	to 3 eyes & mend tongs	.49	Josiah Hayden
	to mend cutter shoe	.18	Andros Gillett
28	to repair cutter sett 2 shoes & mend sleigh	.68	Chester Shelden
29	to iron on neap *	.18	T. Bartlett ·
	to toed 2 sett 2 shoes	.56	Alfred Root
	to ironing sleigh	2.50	Cotton Hayden
30	to mend chains	.10	Andros Gillett
31	to sett 1 tire & nails	.37	Spencer Root
	to 1 new shoe	.31	Joel Hayden
TOTAL		$27.35	

SOURCE: From account book of an unidentified blacksmith, Forbes Library, Northampton, Massachusetts. Of a total of 338 pages, 176 pages are badly damaged, leaving 162 pages intact.

* The tongue of a wagon drawn by two animals.

TABLE 4

SELECTED ENTRIES FROM ACCOUNT BOOK TO SHOW
DIVERSITY OF BLACKSMITH'S SEASONAL WORK

Jan	to mend sleigh	$ .13
	to strap on sled	.17
	to half cord wood	1.25
	to ironing sleigh	2.50
	to half Days by Edwin	.25
	to mend whifeltree	.34
	to iron bob sled	4.50
Feb	to 4 hund & 79 lbs of hay at 1200	2.95
	to 1 cord wood	2.50
Mar	to steel drills	.67
	to iron waggon & neap, sett 2 shoes	3.95
	to mend shovel	.06
	to 2 hooks	.13
	to step to waggon	1.17
Apr	to ironing cart body	2.50
	to ironing 1 sett of Wheels	5.58
	to repair bitt	.06
	to dung fork	1.00
	to repair toast iron	.06
	to ironing whifeltree	.63
	to hoop tub & 2 Dogs	.62
	to nose & fix plow shear	.67
May	to shg hrs sett 4 tires	1.56
	to mend dung fork	.06
	to 9 rake teeth	.17
	to repair bolt	.13
	to mend shingle dog	.18
	to sharp bar fix clevis	.17
	to make & sett cast tin weld hub bands 24 rivets	3.25
Jun	to sett & nail 1 tire	.37
	to 2 washers 2 rivets	1.25
	to sharp 10 drills	.15
	to make 2 bolts	.13
	to mend hoe	.20
	to mend pitch fork	.19
	to ironing bucket	.63

	to repair tongs	.17
	to cart fastener & mend chains	.42
	to one Dash for wagn	1.25
	to laying bar	.25
	to fix steps sett 1 shoe	1.58
	to sharp 3 bars & pick	.30
	to Door hook & Washers	.25
	to mend hinge	.08
	to mend ring & 6 rivets & c.	.34
	to 1 bolt & key for drag	.20
	to mend pump rod	.13
	to make latches & Ketches	1.17
	to mend chain & make lags	.25
Jul	to bolts & wedges & straps	1.50
	to repair wheelbarrow	.37
	to face stone hammer	.75
Aug	look to iron waggon seats	1.17
	to sharp pick	.06
	to one stirrup 4½ lb	.75
	to staple for seat	.25
	to 2 rods 14 inches	.34
	to forging 6 eyes	.75
	to 1 hook 7 links weld 5	.70
	to mend skein to waggon	.04
	to make hoop 14¾"	.04
Sep	to hoop brass kettle	1.00
	to pin & sett 4 tires & nails & hub bands	3.50
	to mend brace to waggon	.06
	to make 2 springs	.13
	to mend saddle	.18
	to one drag tooth 3¾"	.50
	to one hub reamer	1.25
Oct	to make 1 hammer	.18
	hook for boat	.25
	to ironing yoke & whifeltree	2.17
Nov	to work on skales	.25
	to bolt coffee mill	.13
	to iron 2 ladles & 2 rings	.47
	to repair shovel	.16
	to 2 pulley hooks	.33
	to face hammer	.33
	to face hammer	.33
	to upsett 1 axe	.34
	to fix irons to bridge	4.25

1 6 1

Dec	to hay knife & iron	.63
	to ironing cutter & staple	.92
	to head 64 bolts	.32
	to nutts	.13
	to repair bail	.08
	to repair bucket	.06
	to sticking punch	.10

TABLE 5

WEIGHTS OF FLAT IRON BARS, IN POUNDS PER FOOT

WIDTH	THICKNESS				
	¼″	½″	¾″	1″	1½″
1″	.83	1.67	2.50	3.33	5.00
2″	1.67	3.33	5.00	6.67	10.00
4″	3.33	6.67	10.00	13.33	20.00
6″	5.00	10.00	15.00	20.00	30.00

TABLE 6

WEIGHTS OF ROUND, SQUARE, AND OCTAGONAL IRON BARS, IN POUNDS PER FOOT

Dimension	Round	Square	Octagonal
¼″	.164	.208	.1760
½″	.654	.833	.7042
¾″	1.473	1.875	1.5844
1″	2.618	3.333	2.8167
1½″	5.890	7.500	6.337

 Octagonal bar iron is measured between opposite faces.

A Select Bibliography

ASTON, JAMES, and STORY, EDWARD B., *Wrought Iron: Its Manufacture, Characteristics and Application*. Pittsburgh: A. M. Byers Company, 1936.

AYRTON, MAXWELL, and SILCOCK, ARNOLD, *Wrought Iron and Its Decorative Use*. New York: Charles Scribner's Sons, 1929.

BACON, JOHN LORD, *Forge Practice and Heat Treatment of Steel*. New York: John Wiley & Sons, Inc., 1919.

BINING, ARTHUR CECIL, *Pennsylvania Iron Manufacture in the Eighteenth Century*. Harrisburg: Pennsylvania Historical Commission Publications, Vol. 4, 1938.

BOYER, CHARLES S., *Early Forges and Furnaces in New Jersey*. Philadelphia: University of Pennsylvania Press, 1931.

BRIDENBAUGH, CARL, *The Colonial Craftsman*. New York: New York University Press, 1950.

BRITISH WAR OFFICE, *Handbook for Carpenters, Wheelrights, and Smiths*. London: His Majesty's Stationery Office, 1934.

BROOKS, THOMAS R., *Toil and Trouble: A History of American Labor*. New York: Dell Publishing Co., Inc. (Delacorte Press), 1964.

BURLINGAME, ROGER, *March of the Iron Men: A Social History of Union Through Invention*. New York: Charles Scribner's Sons, 1938.

CARRUTH, GORTON, and associates, eds., *The Encyclopedia of American Facts and Dates*. New York: Thomas Y. Crowell Company, 2nd ed., 1959.

CASTERLIN, WARREN S., *Steelworking and Tool Dressing*. New York: M. T. Richardson Company, 1914.

CATHCART, WILLIAM HUTTON, *The Value of Science in the Smithy and Forge*. London: Charles Griffin and Company Ltd., 1920.

CURTI, MERLE, *The Learned Blacksmith: The Letters and Journals of Elihu Burritt*. New York: Wilson-Erickson, 1937.

DOLLAR, JNO. A. W., *A Handbook of Horseshoeing*. New York: Jenkins, 1898.

DREW, JAMES M., *Blacksmithing*. St. Paul Minn.: Redbook Publishing Company, 1935.

FONER, PHILIP S., *History of the Labor Movement in the United States*. New York: International Publishers Co., Inc., 1947.

GEERLINGS, GERALD, *Wrought Iron in Architecture*. New York: Charles Scribner's Sons, 1929.

GOOGERTY, THOMAS F., *Practical Forging and Art Smithing*. Milwaukee, Wis.: Bruce Publishing Company, 1915.

HART, RICHARD H., *Enoch Pratt, the Story of a Plain Man*. Baltimore, Md.: Enoch Pratt Free Library, 1935.

HARTLEY, E. N., *Ironworks on the Saugus*. Norman, Okla.: University of Oklahoma Press, 1957.

HOGG, GARRY, *Hammer and Tongs: Blacksmithery down the Ages*. London: Hutchinson & Co. (Publishers) Ltd., 1964.

HOLMSTROM, JOHN GUSTAF, *American Blacksmithing, Toolsmith's and Steelworker's Manual*. Chicago: Frederick J. Drake, 1916.

————, *Modern Blacksmithing and Horseshoeing*. Chicago: Frederick J. Drake, 1941.

JENKINS, GERANT J., *The English Farm Wagon*. Reading, Berks., England: Oakwood Press for University of Reading, 1961.

JERNBERG, JOHN, *Forging: Manual of Practical Instruction in Hand Forging of Wrought Iron*. Chicago: American Technical Society, 1918.

JONES, LYNN C., *Forging and Smithing: A Book for Schools and for Blacksmiths*. New York: The Century Company, 1924.

KANE, JOSEPH NATHAN, *Famous First Facts*. New York: The H. W. Wilson Co., 3rd ed., 1964.

KAUFFMAN, HENRY J., *Early American Ironware, Cast and Wrought*. Rutland, Vt.: Charles E. Tuttle Company, 1966.

KEITH, HERBERT C., and HARTE, CHARLES RUFUS, *The Early Iron Industry of Connecticut*. New Haven, Conn.: Mack and Noel, 1935.

MITCHELL, EDWIN VALENTINE, *The Horse and Buggy Age in New England*. New York: Coward-McCann, Inc., 1937.

RAWSON, MARION NICHOLL, *Handwrought Ancestors*. New York: E. P. Dutton & Co., Inc., 1936.

RICHARDS, WILLIAM A., *Forging of Iron and Steel*. New York: D. Van Nostrand Co., Inc., 1915.

ROBBINS, FREDERICK W., *The Smith: Traditions and Lore of an Ancient Craft*. London: Rider and Company, 1953.

SCHWARZKAPF, ERNST, *Plain and Ornamental Forging*. New York: John Wiley & Sons, Inc., 1916.

SELVIDGE, R. W., *Blacksmithing: A Manual for Use in School and Shop*. London and New York: Cambridge University Press, 1923.

SONN, ALBERT H., *Early American Wrought Iron*. New York: Charles Scribner's Sons, 1928.

STRAUS, RALPH, *Carriages and Coaches: Their History and Evolution*. New York: J. B. Lippincott Co., 1912.

THRUPP, G. A., *The History of Coaches*. London: Kerby & Endean, 1877.

TUNIS, EDWIN, *Colonial Living*. Cleveland and New York: The World Publishing Company, 1937.

WERTIME, THEODORE, *The Coming of the Age of Steel*. Chicago: The University of Chicago Press, 1962.

WILLIAMSON, SCOTT G., *The American Craftsman*. New York: Crown Publishers, Inc., 1940.

Index